BRUNO BITTERLI-F
DEATH AND L

ra va re

Published by Ravare Books
ravarebooks@gmail.com

Copyright © 2012 by Bruno Bitterli-Fürst

First published in English by Ravare Books 2012
Originally published in Switzerland by Ravare Verlag 2009

Translation by Zambodhi Schlossmacher and Lee Glenn
Edited by Lee Glenn and Zambodhi Schlossmacher
Cover by Bruno Bitterli-Fürst
Photo: © Pefkos–Fotolia.com
Interior design by Tom Gross

ISBN: 978-0-9567040-0-9

BRUNO BITTERLI-FÜRST

Death *and* Life

Table of Contents

Preface

At 32, after considerable training with different yoga teachers and mediums, I experienced a breakthrough: My channel[1] opened and I began receiving daily messages from the spiritual world. Through the unmanifest being of Nicodemus, I received considerable interesting information, assignments, and help with accomplishing earthly challenges. Nicodemus accompanied me as my spiritual teacher for many years. I was very happy that, in addition to myself, this contact benefited the daily and spiritual development of many other people.

This collaboration with the spiritual world resulted in numerous seminars, counseling sessions, and three books. Five years since this radical breakthrough, my view and motivation regarding the spiritual world began to gradually change.

After the publication of the third Enetechiel book, I had had enough of writing and working with the spiritual world. I was disappointed that some of the prophecies had not come true. I felt awful for the people who had trusted me and my channel. In the fullness of time, however, it became clear to me why there are prophecies, and what purpose they fulfill when they don't manifest.

Every person reacts differently to difficult, challenging situations. For me personally, the disappointment concerning the spiritual world initiated a comprehensive grounding process. Up to that point, it had always been far easier for me to have my roots in the spiritual world rather than the material one. But I realized this would not work in the long run and that I no longer wanted it to be so—most especially because the Earth offers us her beautiful land for our use, and gladly receives the roots of those who inhabit it. However, since my childhood, it had always been easier for me to be anchored in the spiritual world rather than the earthly material one. Thus, having suffered significant disappointment in connection with the spiritual world, I was forced to anchor my roots in the Earth. That naturally was no easy process because of preexisting painful experiences ingrained in my being.

For this reason, I needed to transform these old, bitter experiences from the past in order to resolve the separation between my being and the Earth.

To illustrate this with a classic example: When a child burns his hand on the stove, he quickly removes it and avoids contact with the burners again.

The same principle is true regarding experiences with the Earth: People who have frequently 'burned their hands' on the earth through unpleasant experiences, tend to retreat automatically in order to mitigate the pain—a natural, universally protective response.

However, protective instincts often degenerate into fear-based barriers that prevent people from expressing themselves freely and appropriately.

By obtaining a new access to the Earth, its laws, and the love within the Earth, the wish to write another book arose within me. After several approaches and a feeble attempt to find a fitting subject, I put this idea aside again. However, my wish to both write about things that were alive in me, and manifest knowledge, persisted. I wanted to bring the knowledge of my "higher" realms into contact with the Earth.

A few days after I firmly decided on another book project, Elisabeth contacted me from the spiritual world. Elisabeth Kübler-Ross[2]. "Is that really Elisabeth?" I asked myself in the beginning of our encounters. An inner organ developed during the course of my experiences with the spiritual world that I like to call "vibration sensor." Whenever a spiritual being announces itself to me, I feel into it to determine what type of energy quality it is. As it turns out, this has become an invaluable organ. Based on my perception with this organ, I decide whether or not to enter into a conversation. This vibration sensor is also useful for testing the intention of the being that shows up.

In my encounters with Elisabeth, the pendulum was clearly registering on the positive side, and consequently an interesting conversation with her followed in which we began to get to know each other a little.

I did not know Elisabeth during the time she was incarnated, nor had I read any of her books. Apart from Stefan Haupt's film, in which she is portrayed shortly before her "crossing over," I only recall a short newspaper article about her in which she says she worked too much and danced too little in her life.

I liked her immediately in the encounter across the border between our respective worlds, owing to the fact that she did not assume the role of teacher. From the very beginning, we met on a level playing field of equal partnership.

Soon thereafter, the idea presented itself to write a book together. First we had to lay the foundation by establishing some ground rules. For Elisabeth, fun was an important factor, so we agreed that we would dispense with the project if it were no longer fun for either of us. An additional relevant point for me was that we collaborate on the book so that it would be a team effort. I did not want to merely assume the role of medium[3] to allow her to use my body for the production of her book. Because that resonated with her as well, we were soon able to begin.

Compared with other collaborations from the spiritual world, I really enjoyed working with Elisabeth because she was still very close to the Earth. Therefore she was not a lofty contact, but rather one that brought the smell of trees, leaves, and the feel of tax returns with her. She knows what it is like to be incarnated on the earth and to move around in this world. She also knows of the many constraints, numerous challenges, and needs of the body.

Her intimate knowledge of earthly conditions made my work much easier, for it created a natural closeness which I really need for fruitful cooperation. I could also build my trust on this closeness. The boundary between our worlds, as you dear readers certainly also know, is very powerful. Despite the deep satisfaction of breaking through this barrier, despite being deeply moved upon coming into immediate contact with the spiritual world, it takes great strength to ignore the boundaries that have separated generations of human beings from one another. The separation between this side and the other has deeply penetrated both our cellular structure and collective unconscious. Therefore, those who cross these boundaries are skeptically viewed, and often not taken seriously.

It is a Herculean task to challenge the collective myth that holds this side as unequivocally separate from the other, owing to the fact that crossing the border between the worlds does not correspond to anything usual.

It is my intention to cross this border very consciously with the publication of this book. In so doing, it is not to draw attention to myself, but rather to thoroughly break down the boundaries between these worlds at this present time. Up to now, this separation served a very important function by highlighting learning content on earth. Now (and of this, I am certain) it is time to question and penetrate this boundary so that it can be revealed for what it is: An illusion.

On two occasions, I lost the basic element of fun that Elisabeth and I initially agreed as an essential factor in our working together. The first time was when we discussed the text on the cover, because Elisabeth insisted that she be mentioned there too and wanted her full first and last names listed—which I felt very apprehensive about. I suspected there must be something wrong if she had such a need to put herself in the foreground. Such a mature being as she would not be attached to an earthly name.

Now the greatest enemy of this book—doubt—began to draw me into its clutches, which caused me to lose the element of fun for a second time.

At the outset of our work together, my intention was not to mention her name at all in order to keep the focus on the content of the book itself. Furthermore, I did not want to upset either Elisabeth's relatives or fans. Her dry response was: "I am still the one who presides over this name, even if I am no longer present in bodily form. Besides, I have the impression that you overestimate my fame just a little bit."

So, dear reader, if you would now take another look at the front cover, you will see who asserted herself in the end! After considerable thought, it became clear to me that by withholding Elisabeth's name, I would be withholding the truth by omission, and I no longer wished to participate in that divisive dance.

Above all, the fact that this book is a creative collaboration between someone alive in this world (Earth) and someone alive in the next (spiritual) challenges the widely held view that physical death is final. It is also true that Elisabeth Kübler-Ross helped me tremendously in the creation of this book by allowing me to receive large sections of text, and by consistently expressing herself within that information.

Many unknown aspects regarding death and dying came into my conscious awareness through this work. Therefore, I concluded it merits being called what it is: A creative collaboration across the border!

During the time of her earthly life, Elisabeth concerned herself with death. Now she has undertaken this journey herself in full consciousness and describes her experiences. That's why I doubt the statement "No one has ever come back!" This has been widely quoted in discussions involving the theme "what happens after death." It would be more accurate to say: They have returned by the scores already but we could not perceive them because we were only concentrating on the physical body. The physical body definitely does not come back, but the being that has been living in it is frequently trying to make contact again with its loved ones.

There are numerous means of communication in today's age, and so many ways to contact friends and acquaintances, that choosing the right means of communication can be quite a challenge. However, it's worth noting that the quality of communication does not necessarily improve through multiple means.

Channeling[4] is one means of communication among many. By itself, it is neutral—just as writing an email is simply a method for conveying information. However, the quality of energy that flows into the human communication channels at hand is another story. In the beginning of my introduction to the spiritual world, I subconsciously held the opinion that all the information coming to the Earth through channeling had to be true. It has since become clear to me that channeling is just a means of communication, much like a telephone connection.In this regard, it is not so important which means of communication are used, but more importantly, what content is transferred in the communication.

For this reason I recommend that you, dear reader, simply allow the content of this book to sink in, use your vibration sensor, and allow yourself to feel whether these texts enrich you. In my opinion, that is essential. It is my wish for channeling to become a natural means of communication, neither under nor over valued—and thus a component of communication in our society. My wish also embraces the notion that including another dimension both broadens and enriches life, and presents a whole new outlook vs. the notion that what is channeled must be true—for that is always very idiosyncratic.

It was very stimulating for me to feel Elisabeth's support as I was writing. She has a wonderful capacity to go straight to the heart of an issue without any hesitation, and without being sharp or hurtful—a quality I gladly integrate into my own repertoire.

The encounters with her when not engaged in writing the book were very moving for me because, even though she no longer lives in a physical body, the search for truth and the challenges that present themselves are also felt in the spiritual world. At times she also reached her limits, as she had to move back and forth from one world to another. We always worked at the same time in the evenings, because then the chances were best that I would not be disturbed working. So for a long time she "traveled" to me on a daily basis.

Be happy that challenges don't stop when the cycle of incarnation[5] comes to an end and the transition to the realm of the archangels takes place. Conditions of exhaustion exist there too, and other experiences that are right on the edge of being excessively demanding. That was made abundantly clear to me as I was working with Elisabeth.

And I must say, that knowledge makes the matter all the more attractive to me. The other side is neither Heaven nor Hell, but rather learning experiences that continue. This is in the sense of infinitely ongoing development alongside the wish to come closer and closer to God within oneself.

If you let yourself be open to the contents of this book, and can let yourself be touched by these lines, a transformative process will be automatically set in motion.

Try to be as relaxed as possible when reading it. Take your time, and your relationship to death will change. Perhaps some painful past experiences, or restrictive patterns kept alive through collective unconscious, will surface into your conscious awareness. Ultimately, these conditions all contribute to healing your ideas about death.

I wish you much joy in your transformation, and fun

with the encounter of life that follows death, with Elisabeth who has already gone through the tunnel of death and brings us interesting information from the world beyond, and in the encounter with yourself.

I have chosen to omit which parts of this book are channeled from Elisabeth and which are mine. However, within the dialogues, it is clearly specified. It is Elisabeth who is the main source of the texts. There are also texts that resulted from merging our energies—the so—called Teamwork Texts.

In the spiritual world, the dividing line between individuals is not as clear as in the material world. I have accounted for this fact by not declaring every text by name.

Please note that for reasons of simplification, I have used the masculine form throughout—although this term assumes both masculine and feminine. I have also written the book using a familiar format for a simple reason: In these frequencies, there is no longer a formal distance between souls, such as that expressed in more conventional formats. These are soul levels wherein we are all close, where we all have similar problems, and where we are ultimately not really separated.

With warmest personal regards,

Bruno Bitterli-Fürst

_____

I am very happy to reach you now in this way, dear readers. Ever since my earthly incarnation, I have worked very closely with dying, death, and what comes afterward. In the meantime, I have made this journey through death myself, and am beginning to feel at home on the other side, as I am gradually getting used to the so-called *hereafter*.

I have chosen Bruno as a medium because it feels right from where I am; because what I want to say comes through clearly; and because additionally we can learn a few things from each other. I can learn about dedication from Bruno; and Bruno can learn how to write books from me.

Relationships that reach beyond the limits of earthly life are also based on the principle of give and take. And here, too, it is about meaningful exchange.

In this book, dear reader, I would like to embark upon a path with you that touches on themes such as death in connection with life, death during life, and what really happens when the physical body dies. I am very happy you are joining me on this journey, that swings from the here-and-now to the hereafter; happy that the borders between these worlds are thereby getting thinner and thinner and more permeable, so they eventually disappear completely.

Elisabeth Kübler-Ross

Part I

DEATH–TRANSFORMATONS MOST POWERFUL FORCE

DYING

Usually a process involving some time precedes death, which is called dying. Dying can last two days, two seconds, or even two months or more. Dying is the actual preparation for death, and death is correspondingly influenced by the preceding dying process.

If death has been well prepared for by a conscious dying process, then it is the most natural thing in existence. However, if fear is a main factor in the dying process, then it affects the transition through death's gate.

It is important that the dying process receives exactly the same attention as the birth process. When a new life comes into being, it is very easy for a person to turn his whole attention to this wonderful process of creation.

But when life is about to evaporate and separate from its old form, the person tends to turn away and draw his attention back. Small children are easily nourished by the overflowing enthusiasm, care, and love of their fellow human beings. Older people, whose life light is slowly extinguishing, hardly receive any attention at all. Discomfort, fear, and a form of sorrow generally surround their death.

But in actuality, death paves the way for new life; and the way in which we meet death is the way in which we meet life in its depth! That is why I plead for a new kind of attention toward the dying process. If death is seen as that which it really is—namely, thorough preparation for life in a new outfit—then dying is put in its proper perspective.

Until now, mainly loss, sorrow, pain, and perhaps even relief (if a great deal of suffering was involved) have been associated with dying. Whoever finds it possible to regard death as preparation for a new life, can count himself lucky.

An example: Ben had been yearning to leave Earth for a very long time. Suicide, he knew, wouldn't get him anywhere. His soul already had this experience, and knew that it just delayed the soul's developmental and maturation process. Therefore, he often prayed at night to simply fall asleep and not wake up in the morning.

His inner guidance saw things very differently, however. It knew that a few more lessons were needed, and that it would not be to the soul's satisfaction if Ben's wish were granted. And so, Ben's *Higher Self* decided to confront Ben with dying so that the preparatory work for death could already begin. For in this current incarnation, Ben's soul wanted to experience a conscious transition from this world to the other.

So Ben got sick. After lengthy examination, his doctor's prognosis was that he probably had only two or three more years to live. That was a tough blow for Ben. His ability to move freely lessened daily, wearing him down considerably. That was exactly what he did not want: A slow dying process in which his ability for action would be increasingly limited. Actually, he would have preferred just the opposite: A quick transition to the other realm and, ideally, at night.

A huge conflict began to brew in Ben, because from his earthly human self he wanted to end his incarnation. And now he had the impression with this prognosis that death was approaching bit by bit rather than all at once. This thought deterred him completely. And so in the beginning, he fought with all his might against the myriad constraints imposed on him by his illness. Again and again he came to his edge by overdoing it, and subsequently paid a high price by being confined to his bed for longer periods of time.

In the course of time his resistance weakened, and he was able to recognize that his quality of life suffered greatly when he constantly ignored the limits set by his body. So he decided to be kinder and more loving to himself and to his destiny. And, as a result of his decision, a foundation was formed that allowed him to be immeasurably creative. From the viewpoint of the soul, a very valuable process began—the dying process.

You are probably feeling sad, dear readers, that Ben didn't fight for his survival and do everything under the sun to change his situation and outsmart death. Yet exactly by going along with the destiny that he had chosen for himself on some level of his being, he created the opportunity to come into even deeper contact with *life*.

Ben surrendered to his situation, lay down when his body had no more strength, and contacted his inner self. There, he often found a relentlessly tangled web: Fear and hope shifted back and forth in a fierce battle, taking a great deal of the remaining energy Ben still had at his disposal. Therefore, he decided to get in touch with a therapist who might be able to help him create order in his inner being. His relationships with his mother and father were examined in these sessions. And so time and again Ben touched his past with his spirit and uncovered the connections within his biography.

That did him considerable good. For until that point, he would act out his unresolved problems with various drugs and escapades with women, until he stood before a rubble heap time and again. And, as mentioned before, he wanted to die; or, respectively, escape.

Nothing came of escaping or dying the way he imagined it would. His inner guidance now accompanied him through the dying process more and more. Yet it was quite different from what he had imagined. The confrontations with his illness, and his greatly reduced ability to be active, kept raising the question of what he really wanted. Through this inner confrontation, he realized that many of his ideas about life had repeatedly led him into painful situations with no way out—and had thus inflicted deep wounds.

"How can I be free of all this baggage of old ideas, injuries, and conditioning?" he asked himself. And the idea came to him that *he could quite simply just let all those ideas die.*

This was, after he had surrendered to his situation, the second significant turning point in his life: He understood that the main thing for him now was not to escape, leave his body behind, and find solace in a nonmaterial existence, but to realize that he had the possibility to accompany *aspects* of his being that no longer served him to their death!

ACCOMPANYING ASPECTS
OF ONE'S BEING INTO DEATH

Ben suspected that in this way, he could free himself of loads of baggage: That he could in fact release material he had carried in his earthly backpack day in and day out; and that, by so doing, he could free himself from an enormous burden.

A joy for life began to grow within him; a joyful anticipation—the likes of which he had not experienced since his first day of school. He was happy to think that he didn't have to go away, instead the obstructive aspects of his being were allowed to die and he would be even more wakefully present as a result.

His new motto became: "Accompany old aspects of my being into death." A very challenging task that required much from him. For every time he delved into an aspect of his being and found that it no longer had any useful purpose, he began to fear that when this aspect died, he (Ben) would follow this aspect into death.

By allowing the death of an aspect of his being to occur several times, his fear began to gradually dissipate. Each time he was able to be more fully present; and soon he realized that, after death, even more life is available than beforehand.

In this manner, his inner guidance had brought him to a point that corresponded with a very deep soul wish. His doctors were amazed when he became more mobile, contrary to their professional prognoses. With a light heart, he was able to take on new tasks.

Ben had learned everything there was for him to learn from this illness—and with that, his inner guidance had ended this "curriculum." With Ben's example, I want to illustrate that every person is at once the one who dies, and the one who accompanies dying.

DEATH IN EVERYDAY LIFE

Everyday life is an especially wonderful measure for dealing with death. Here death appears in many different ways:

- Handling waste
- Beloved pets and their death
- Situations to which I am mentally attached
- Shifts in family structure
- Changes in work
- Changes in the body (getting older)

- Changes in furniture / home remodeling
- Emotional attachments to people, situations and conditions
- Dealing with depression and loss of strength
- Loss of material goods

Just take a look at the above-mentioned events in your everyday life. Of course we could make it even more poignant and say that every moment is dying in order to make room for each subsequent moment. Yet this occurs within such a subtle frequency, that we need to first examine death in more palpable terms.

PARALLELS BETWEEN DEATH & WASTE

Every living system contains qualities that can be described on the one hand as growing, and on the other hand as dying. Viewed from a simple physical perspective, every household has several trash cans and waste paper baskets. A healthy household accounts for both acquiring and disposing of things at the appropriate time. A human being's energetic system functions in much the same way: Acquisition and disposal.

Interestingly enough, aspects that have to do with disposal acquire much less attention and social prestige than aspects that are responsible for production. Just take a look at the social status of the waste industry. Morgues are enveloped in the same aura of uniqueness and mystery today as they were in the past. And hearses hold a particularly special fascination for people.

On a material level, the entire disposal industry has a lot to do with the theme of death: An object that is no longer needed is disposed of and usually buried or burned. A change of form takes place. These outer phenomena find their correspondence in every person's energy system. Many books are written about the art of cooking, the production of food and about the most diverse creations. Yet, what concerns itself with it's disposal—what about digestion in the human body? These are tangential themes. Yet digestion and nutritional utilization have exactly the same value as the creation of food. But digestion has to do with death, and is therefore moved to the back of the line as a topic of conversation.

Just recently, global disregard of death has shown up in the fact that chemical landfills have to be dug out because they are mutating into ticking time bombs. Or whole regions had been affected by the lack of planning for refuse. And as a result, waste was left lying in heaps on the street.

A wonderful picture for the challenge: "Please, ladies and gentlemen, take a look at your own waste. Confront yourselves with this, please. For it is an essential part of human life, and there is much to be gained from understanding it. The handling of waste is a yardstick for the handling of death."

Not only are there people who accompany other people to their death, there are people who also accompany matter to its death. Basically it is one and the same thing.

Death is "just" the transition for birth into a new structure, new composition, and newly created energy.

THE TRUE COMPANION OF DYING

The true companion of dying is not a person who has a lot of ideas about everything that might happen after death. The true companion of dying is a person who has already died during his lifetime on earth without leaving his body!

Ultimately, dying within an incarnation cannot be described. It can only be experienced. Ask yourself the following:

- Are you really ready to die?
- If you were about to die, what would you miss?
- What would you miss, if it would die?

A person tends to focus on loss in connection with death. If he manages to get through these feelings of loss—with courage and determination—then the foundation for a new life is laid that much faster.

REPERCUSSIONS OF FEAR

The toughest, most unyielding 'force' that hinders, prolongs and creates a pitiful scenario for dying is fear. Fear dampens and delays the process of dying to such a degree that it can barely be comprehended with human perception. If fear is the lead element in the dying process (and by that I mean the dying of aspects of the personality as well as the dying that eventuates in leaving one's physical body, then fear will cause the dying process to last two to four times longer. It would be completely different if the in-depth knowledge about death as a life-enhancing experience were the underlying concept.

These are facts that are observed from the spiritual realm. Fear is what turns dying into a horror story that so many people are afraid of: The deadly cycle of fear, experienced in the flesh.

THE INTERPLAY OF DEATH & LIFE

In actuality, death stands completely in service to life. While there is frequent confusion surrounding this statement, death is not life's adversary. On the contrary, death *serves* life because it consumes everything that life no longer needs for its perpetuation and progress. Consequently, death is not life's enemy, but rather life's friend. As such, humankind is truly challenged to awaken to a new and open-minded viewpoint toward death.

Death is a living part of life because it actively supports the dynamic of change that underlies all of life. For example, the soul might announce, "We no longer need the aspects termed *despair* and *resignation*." Therefore, what instrument might most effectively remove these aspects from the human field? Death.

Someone who knows (and is in touch with) himself, can hear the call of his own soul. Of his own accord, he can surrender resignation and despair to be transformed through the use of meditation and visualization techniques. These useless energy forms are thus converted and now available as renewed energy, readily accessible to the soul who transformed them.

Whoever maintains a fear-free attitude around the transformative power of death has a great advantage, because dying time for the various aspects will thereby be shortened considerably. Successful dying could sound like this:

- I sense that an aspect of my being is ready for death (transformation).
- I accompany this aspect to the point of death (transformation) with gratitude and joy.
- Strengthened and fulfilled, I can now give myself more deeply to the reality of life.

It isn't about joining the spirit of our time and pulling out all the stops, misusing the powers modern man has acquired in order to elude death. Nor is it about playing a game of hide-and-seek with death—which death would ultimately win anyway. This is also not about forcefully protecting life from death. Instead, it's about successfully accompanying useless aspects of one's own being to their death—with dignity.

DEATH–LIFE

If we ask someone what the opposite of death is, he will most likely say life. If we ask the reverse, what's the opposite of life, he will most likely answer death. But life has no opposite, because life includes everything there is—even death!

If we view death as the opposite of life, then it will always be something to avoid. Who would like to enter into no-mans-land with the knowledge that he or she might stay there forever? Every being has the right to eternal life; and no one has the right to be the way he now is forever. No one has the right to keep the form that he now has for all eternity. That would be absurd, for it would go against the fundamental laws of evolution—which are an essential part of life. What am I leading up to?

If death can be put in its proper place—where it rightfully belongs—then death changes immediately. But if I associate death with loss, fear, and view it as irreversible, then my transition to the nonmaterial world will be affected by these attributes. However, if I am able to see death differently while alive—that is, as a great transmuter of useless aspects; if I can view death as a bridge to another form of being, then it might even be possible for me to transition in a relaxed, joyful, and loving manner.

The purpose of this book, dear reader, is really only to present you with the possibility that dying—all the way to physical death—can be something wonderful. And if you are able to view dying as one of the most exciting experiences life offers, then death will no longer appear as your adversary, but instead, as your ally. Yet, as is so often the case, there is one pre-condition to the process of dying joyfully—namely: Disengage death, or the idea of death, from fear—absolutely and completely.

Now the questions arise: How do I do that? Are there concrete methods that will support me in comprehending just how strongly death and fear are intertwined with one another within me? And how can I release this entanglement?

This is a very pivotal, even life-altering, question—especially in light of the fact that one's attitude towards death significantly determines one's quality of life.

HOW DO I SEPARATE DEATH FROM FEAR?

As already mentioned, the union between fear and death is one of the most destructive bonds there is on Earth. By itself, fear alone is really powerful. Now just imagine how heavy and influential it becomes when allied with death. It has to be said in advance that there are very few of us living on earth today who are not affected by the enmeshment of fear and death. Most people have this configuration deep within themselves and regard it as something quite natural. Most people believe fear and death belong together naturally.

I say: Yes, although it is the case with most people, it still doesn't make it natural in point of fact. Natural is when people successfully navigate the death and dying process without fear.

In this regard, there is quite a bit of work to be done. This work could be titled: What does my preparation for a truly natural death look like? What do I have to do to be truly free and relaxed throughout the process of dying?

Imagine an existence, dear reader, in which death is not constantly lurking behind every door waiting to annihilate everything that exists. Instead, imagine an existence where death is a wonderful ally, a powerful architect for life's highest quality, rather than an adversary. While death does indeed remove what currently exists, it also enables the creation of something entirely new in its stead.

We still have not resolved the question of how to disentangle the association between fear and death. I have already given one important clue: To allow myself to revise my ideas of death. To give myself the chance to see death in another light. And rather than emphasize what is being taken away, focus on that which now becomes possible through death. This doesn't necessarily mean the dying process will be painless. But it does mean that fruitless and unproductive resistance against death can be eliminated, along with any resulting procrastination.

Another very effective method is to research how death is connected to fear through our lineage. Were my Grandparents afraid to die? What images influenced them?

What did they imagine life after death to be like? On the one hand, this can be done very practically, by simply seeking out conversations with relatives and bringing up the subject. It can also be accomplished through family constellation work [as developed by Bert Hellinger], whereby the field of ancestors is set up in order to lift it into the realm of consciousness. For example, a grandmother who was terribly afraid of dying influences a grandchild far more than was previously assumed.

Ancestors not only prepare the way *to* Earth, they also prepare the way *from* Earth. In this sense, the conscious work you do regarding the dying and death process is not only for you, it is also for your descendants.

People who calmly and peacefully (and perhaps even joyfully) cross the threshold into the nonmaterial world represent bright pillars of light in the landscape of families and whole world structures. From the point of view of a being who is no longer incarnate, this is a lot easier for me to see now.

Furthermore, dear reader, you can let the word "death" resonate within yourself and notice what happens. Does everything tighten up inside your body? Or is it possible for you to just let it be and see that death can exist as a very natural instrument within you?

Death is not poisonous; death is something that happens daily. Death is constantly present, but if it is continuously ignored, a lot of energy is needed to flee from it. Many projects, many unnecessary movements occur day in and day out with just one simple motivation:

Fear of death.

What then does man do out of fear of death?

- Man erects memorials—out of fear of death.
- Man suppresses others—out of fear of death.
- Man lives out of the forces of the ego—out of fear of death.
- Man cannot allow any love in—out of fear of death.
- Man is afraid of oneself—out of fear of death.
- Man cannot trust others—out of fear of death.
- Man cannot trustingly engage with others—out of fear of death.
- Man cannot trustingly engage with himself—out of fear of death.

The list could go on and on because the fear of death is so deeply ingrained in our roots. It is so entrenched, that it is widely accepted as something inevitable, something that could not possibly be viewed otherwise.

And that is precisely the point, and why I wish to help you create the following paradigm shift from within: Death is nothing terrible. Death is not final with regard to eternity; death is, and remains, a valuable and powerful transition.

With these words I can only accompany you as far as the gates of your own ideas about death. Only you can bring into consciousness that which exists in your mind under the heading of death. These words are merely meant to highlight how and where you might discover for yourself how comfortable (or uncomfortable) your view of death is. They are merely a guidepost intended to assist you explore your idea of death. How it feels from within. How well it fits. Most of all, how it feels to carry it forward (or not) as you move through life.

In the end, death is a territory in which every inhabitant of earth walks. Yet, there are different levels of awareness and comfort. In this respect, the awareness that I have raised completely into my consciousness is the most comfortable fit. When I have really become conscious of death, I am able to put this construct to use for my highest good. Then I am no longer the constant victim of my own ideas or fear of death.

DEATH—AN INSTRUMENT OF LIFE

If I know that death is an instrument of life—an instrument that guarantees evolution and consciousness—then I will have the opportunity to anchor myself even more deeply in human existence. To begin with, I will also be able to know that everything is relative; and secondly, everything is just a matter of time, as it all has to pass through death's door eventually.

Nothing existing on Earth as visible matter can escape death. Everything—absolutely everything—is destroyed by death. Of course I can view this fact however I want: "Too bad that everything is mortal" is one variation; "Great, everything is subject to continuous transformation" is another. The most helpful version for the long term could be: "I accept that on earth, an ongoing, joyful change takes place; and that everything, except love, undergoes death."

Love is the power that does not have to go through death, because death was created out of love. Love is older and truer than death. But that is only incidental.

DEATH, LOVE & DYING

From the moment love, death, and dying merge, and a union of these three elementary energy forms results, separation is overcome. Put another way: Death is integrated as that which it really is. Of course that takes time. But it's worth mentioning again, because that is the actual goal: Overcoming the barrier between love and death.

These seemingly opposing powers merge into one power. Death is integrated. Death finds its place in the All-That-Is.

Yet for the moment, a few events need to be examined more closely. A prerequisite for the successful integration of an aspect is that whatever has separated the energies has to be eliminated. Painful experiences are what have separated the energy of death and the energy of love. Whosoever is willing (and feels the desire within) to bring love and death together, will not be able to avoid raising the painful wall of separation between these two aspects into consciousness. Because this practice can bring up pain, many people shy away from taking this task in hand. That is why many people have *reactions* to the events around death, rather than thinking them through beforehand. That is regrettable, because this refusal to be concerned with death expends a great amount of life force. This may sound illogical, but it is absolutely true. For as has already been stated, death is not an adversary of life; but instead it is a perfect organizer of transformation, a skilled waste collector, and preparation for new things yet to come!

WHAT DOES THE BARRIER BETWEEN
LOVE & DEATH CONSIST OF?

The barriers that separate death and love into two opposite poles consist of many images and ideas originating
from painful experiences which are stored on the soul
level, as well as in the highly traumatic separation between God and man.

Man usually believes in death as an authority that is
capable of *completely* eradicating a human being. Just
imagine the scope of this! With this idea—being *completely wiped out*—everyone becomes afraid of death. How
does a person even arrive at this notion of being totally
wiped out?

With this question in mind, we inevitably reach the subject of separation between God and man. Someone who
is connected to the divine also experiences God within his
being—in his heart; and hence, also in his outer world. He
does not experience separation between God and himself
anymore; he experiences himself as a divine being; and as

a result, no longer has the idea of being completely extinguished. Only in the falsely perceived absence of God does death appear as something final.

That is precisely what makes death so cruel, so merciless, and so irrevocably final. From this point of view, death is not integrated in God (life) as an important component and regenerator, but is seen as a powerful and eventual killer—able to do away with life without further ado; and, as such, constitutes the polar opposite of life. Within this perspective, death must be feared, because no one likes to be completely eliminated. At least, not the majority of people. Final extinction does not correspond to the principle of life. Final extinction speaks to the belief in the supremacy of death. And that comes about because there is no access to the divine.

DEATH THAT IS INTEGRATED IN GOD

Death that is integrated in God has a completely different quality. If I am conscious of myself and know that life will continue in some form after death then I can die more relaxed. If I assume that life is definitely over after death, then logically something is going to struggle against this so-called *final* death. The dying and death principle is embedded in the knowledge of eternal life, and death may be welcomed in the knowledge that blessings will grow from its presence.

DEATH AS A PREREQUISITE FOR LIFE

E: Dear Bruno, what dying processes have you already undergone?

B: I keep dying over and over again. Said another way: Aspects of myself are always dying—relationships that die, favorite situations that die, ideas about the way life should be that die. There are very many areas in which I have experienced dying. I used to be less conscious of the dying process, which made it more difficult—especially as it brought considerable fear and difficulty in letting go.

During the course of numerous inner processes, a habituation effect came into being regarding dying. Along with that, trust grew in the healing effects of dying. It went so far with me that I began to crave pushing aspects to their death in order to allow something new to come in.

E: Most people cling tightly to life because they have not

learned to die. And because they have not learned to die, they are not able to really live. That is the core point. As a precondition, real life requires the ability to be able to die. This is so for the simple reason that death is a component of life. Death is an aid for real living. Death makes room for that which is new. Death frees us from that which has become old. Death deletes the uncomfortable. Death demolishes what is useless. From this perspective, death is nothing but a blessing. Now unfortunately, people hate death because from their point of view, it causes another separation. From the earthly perspective, leaving the body is seen as going into the unknown. It is understandable that people fear death and are fed up with having to endure further separation from their loved ones, including sharing enjoyable habits and relying on predictable physical laws.

The wish to experience death in a new way can be expressed in the following mantra: "I would like to experience death as that which it actually is. It is a blessing; it is the bearer of freedom; and it is quite simply good."

As already mentioned: Only the person who is really able to die, is able to live.

FEAR & DEATH

Let's look at this subject again, so that we can continue. Fear and death are a duo on earth whose combination has the most serious consequences. Fear alone already weighs people down. Combined with death, they are an almost unbeatable pair. What is my point? Death extinguishes, death removes, death separates—seemingly.

Yet fear is the power that prevents movement, that brings energy to a standstill, that throttles the flow of energy and puts the brakes on—slowing down separation and delaying departure.

You see, for some people there is an attraction to the notion that (through fear) their death is delayed. Death and fear are a paired synonym for decelerating death and drawing it out. For many people this is very interesting, as it allows them to harbor the illusion that this way they will live longer. But the problem lies in the fact that delaying death doesn't create *more* life, instead it lengthens a miserable life of reduced quality.

I maintain that true life only takes place when death is not ignored, pushed to one side, or kept under cover. True life takes place when death is integrated into life.

From a certain point on in the development of a spiritually advanced person, death is invited independently and voluntarily when its time has come. This is because a corresponding inner maturity is present along with the awareness that death is an important component of the healing plan for Earth, and thereby for oneself.

DEATH

Countless people die annually, just as yearly, daily, and hourly innumerable people come into the world. It is an endless coming and going. Although being born and dying are the most natural things in the world, birth and death are handled in entirely different ways. Being born is a joyful event and dying is a mournful event.

Of course taking leave is sorrowful, and it is painful when a beloved person changes planes. But the sometimes huge drama that takes place when someone changes from a material form of existence to the nonmaterial dimension is not necessary to this degree. Why not?

The person who is in mourning (who has just "lost" someone very dear) usually assumes that this person is no longer present. And viewed this way it is indeed very painful and distressing. However, if the mourner finds it possible to imagine that the person who has just changed to another form of existence is generally even *more* present than before, then a whole new reality arises. Because the departed being is no longer attached to the body, immense capabilities arise.

Due to my bodily presence on Earth being rather recent, it is very touching for me to see how actively spiritual beings influence the material world and incarnated beings.

The family ties do not disintegrate because one of its members has changed to another dimension. On the contrary, the connection often intensifies for the beings that have "crossed over." This is due to the many responsibilities connected to bodily life that are suddenly no longer present: No face that has to be washed, no body that has to be nourished, no sleep that is necessary, and so on. All that comes to an end when the body is left behind. You can imagine how much freedom and "time" are suddenly available when the life force no longer has to stream into these daily activities. What do the beings do, who in this case have sufficient capabilities? For example, they write books, either for the nonmaterial world or for the material world—just as I am doing at this moment.

I have written many books during my incarnation, and you can't imagine how much fun I am now having writing through the body and the finer structures of a being who is still incarnated. For one thing, since leaving my body, my point of view has broadened enormously; and for another, I am no longer bound to the written and unwritten duties that are customary among people. Through this, a massive creative potential arises. Even more, there is the possibility for coming closer to the creator, as creativity occurs from a place of love. That often catapults me into a state of highest ecstasy. It also makes me euphoric knowing that it is now possible to discuss the subject of death from my current form of existence. And, in the best case scenario, I can offer you the chance to benefit from my experiences as I share them from the "other side."

RECONCILIATION WITH DEATH

Death is the real form of fear. Even though death is the master of deep metamorphosis, people are afraid of it. Should one have the good fortune of being able to *flow* through death in a relaxed and trusting manner, then death is the most wonderful means of transformation there is. Whenever possible, the average person avoids confrontation with death and usually tries to create an existence in which he simply feels good with what is available to him. In the best-case scenario, he is able to function with what his ancestors (mother, father, grandparents) have left to him. Considering the numerous and complex challenges that are now coming to humankind in its current developmental phase, the solutions given by ancestors are simply no longer enough. The signs of the present time are very clear and point to urgent transformation. The ancestors' "toolbox" is no longer valid in this climate of extreme inner challenges. Humans have such huge demands placed on them these days, that they need additional tools. One of the main tools that needs to be used is *reconciliation with death*!

Reconciling with death is not a task that is only necessary when a physical departure is imminent. Rather, it is more important to reconcile with death in the midst of earthly life. When death no longer brings up fear, and when fear does not unnecessarily and painfully prolong the time of death (of an aspect of one's being), then a powerful life force, a resounding "yes" to life, comes into being that cannot be achieved in any other way.

Reconciliation with death is much more comprehensive than accepting the truth that everyone must die. Reconciling with death is a path that can be traveled everyday. Death is everywhere, and it takes place more often and comprehensively than is commonly perceived.

EVERY MOMENT DIES

The death process begins at the point at which I dive into time, for what exists now, no longer exists ten seconds later. The most recent moment has already died. It is now dead. Through remembering, I can breathe a little life into it. But it is no longer the same in remembrance as it was when it actually happened. For this reason, the dying process is constantly taking place. Whoever is not able to really die, is not able to totally live and love!

DEATH AS A FOUNDATION FOR NEW LIFE

Imagine if nature brought forth plants that would never rot. A terrible scenario: Trees that were uprooted by a storm, branches that fell in a forest, fruit peels—all this would not rot. Imagine the scene: The compost piles would have to be infinitely extended, the surface of the Earth would grow a few millimeters every day, grass would grow and grow and would be indestructible. Embedded in this simple illustration is the blessing of impermanence. Because that which is no longer needed starts to decompose independently, a highly important process is introduced: The dying process could also simply be called transformation process. It's the same thing. The energy that the formation required—for example, a banana peel—recedes and thereby becomes available for some new matter-forming processes.

What am I trying to say with this analogy? Dying and the closure of dying (death) lay a foundation out of which new life can arise. The more a person braces himself against the process of dying and death, the more he hinders the creation and formation of fresh, new life.

This is why I don't think much of the numerous life-prolonging measures that are used with such intensity —which seem to me rather contemptuous of human beings. Raising the quality of existence on Earth is human. Artificially prolonging the quantity that is, the number of years (also of truly unworthy human existence) seems cruel to me. Cruel because the natural process of dying is slowed down, owing mostly to a very basic motivation: Fear of death!

When life-extending measures are used for someone (regardless of whether that life is no longer worth living); and if using these measures is due to fear of death, then new karma is created. Fear always creates karma. Painful experience can dissolve the energy of karma, but it would be false to believe that painful experience forces karmic energy to dissolve.

(Actually, I don't particularly like to use the term karma, because like many other words, it carries so much baggage, and often calls forth additional ideas. It seems to me that the term enmeshed energy would be more appropriate.)

BEING FORCED TO CONFRONT DEATH

Fear of death has many far-reaching consequences. The branches rooted in the fear of death are very diverse and of heavy consequence, yet rarely can a person grasp the entire extent regarding this fear of death during his incarnation. Normally, a person lives out his fear of death by ignoring it and occupying himself with everything else that definitely has nothing to do with death. That works only until one's inner guidance creates a situation in which avoidance is no longer possible.

For example:

Eric received the diagnosis of cancer. It was a tremendous shock, for he only went to the doctor because of a stomachache he had had for a long time. As the Doctor informed him of his diagnosis, Eric's entire life philosophy, his values, and his goals all collapsed within very short order. Many values that were extremely important to him and activities that brought meaning to his life crumbled in no time—in light of the fact that he would soon no longer exist.

Eric went through an intensive process, resulting in the important and unimportant things in his life clearly separating themselves from each other. He realized that the relationship with his wife meant much more to him than he had previously thought. His career, which he had successfully pursued and built up, immediately faded into the background and became almost insignificant. He began to intensely examine the subject of what might happen to him after death. He read about near-death experiences.

Although many of his values basically fell apart with a bang, within a very short time he was not able to connect with his deep inner life plan.

A great emptiness arose that often did not allow him to sleep. In the wee hours, when he tossed and turned in bed while everything was quiet around him, many thoughts went through his head. Above all, he became increasingly aware of his fear of death. At first he felt this fear as a nagging, painful tightness that came up because he was to leave behind his so carefully and practically arranged life. He was afraid that everything he was so accustomed to would be taken away from him all at once. He didn't know whether he loved his life or not—but he was used to it. Of this he was sure.

So, during one of his especially exhausting sleepless

nights, he asked himself "What is making me so afraid of death, or of the thought of death?" At first he simply couldn't come up with anything. He could not answer this question. But he knew (based on his bodily reactions) that sometimes this fear was growing into a monster that was almost squeezing him to death. "What is it that makes me so afraid of death?" "What is it about death that makes me so afraid?" he kept asking himself over and over.

Only after he'd asked himself this question repeatedly during countless nights of sleeplessness, did the force of his fear begin to abate somewhat. He suspected that this question could only be met with partial answers. A considerable partial answer lay in the fact that he had absolutely no idea what was supposed to happen afterwards. Sure, he had heard of the striking reports that told of what people had experienced when their bodies had been declared clinically dead and they then came back to life. But he really hadn't been able to relate to those reports up to now.

But now he saw himself confronted with a situation in which he had to seriously look at this phenomenon. The only thing he could do was to confront the situation inwardly. The moment he would have to let go of everything on earth was getting closer day by day. The probability that he could return to the life he was used to living was destroyed by his diagnosis. A further answer to the question why he had such a great fear of death lay in the fact that he was not yet ready at all to let go of the circumstances in which he now found himself - especially not from his relationship to his wife.

Eric found himself in a situation as so often happens. Someone who has been relatively successful in life is surprised with a life-threatening diagnosis and is hopelessly overwhelmed. Overwhelmed because he had never contemplated death. Until the moment of his diagnosis, his focus was primarily on making himself as comfortable as possible according to worldly standards. The "why" and "wherefore" of things had never really interested him, for everything in his life had gone reasonably well.

The diagnosis of cancer put him into a state of shock. He was confused, and became aware that wherever possible he had avoided death. Several years ago, when his mother had become seriously ill, it wasn't until later that he noticed that his desire to visit her had been drastically reduced. And he also thought that those who found themselves in a difficult situation had caused it themselves.

In the meantime, in his new condition, he was at times very angry with his body—which no longer functioned at all in the way he wanted it to. Not only had he lost control over his body, but he also lost control over his life. And that was much worse.

IN DEATH'S FIRM GRIP

As I have already emphasized, death is a state of transition. It is no monster, no beast that wants to scare or terrorize human beings. Yet, death develops into all of this when it is ignored, fought against, or not seen as that which it actually is: The strongest transformer that exists!

Why has death become something that, as an analogy, goes through the world as the Grim Reaper, carrying a scythe, hunting for seemingly random victims to prove his power over them?

Death is a unique and powerful process that seeks its counterpart. However, and this is the crucial point: Death is not powerful in a destructive sense, but in a transformative sense.

Death is capable of separating a person in just a few seconds from that which has become dear to him during his earthly life: His fellow human beings, his material belongings, his human habits, his culture—in short, everything that is important to him.

Does the Grim Reaper really mow everything down with a sweep of its scythe? Does nothing at all remain when he goes to work, possibly casting his eye specifically on me simply because I have received the diagnosis "incurable illness"?

Here is the crux of the matter and what our observation is all about: Am I only living in the realm of external senses and putting great value on the collection of material goods (in which I include relationships to other people)—if the answer is yes, then death does indeed rip everything away. Then the Grim Reaper lives up to his reputation and eliminates my whole being. I am completely snuffed out. "Yes, the Grim Reaper with the scythe has me totally in his grip now, and with his coming everything is taken away from me." Seen in this way, it is understandable when fear unites with death and the dying process.

WHO IS NOT AFRAID OF THE GRIM REAPER?

There are probably very few people who have *no* fear of death. Why, then, are there people who have no fear of death? What is the reason that some people are able to look death calmly in the face, receive it with dignity, maybe even welcome it, in order to finally move through it?

They believe in God! Is it enough to believe in God, to be able to enter the dying process without fear? Is it possible that there is no God after all; that after I step through death's door, I step into an endless nothing, and gradually dissolve into nothing, and that I am extinguished forever and ever? Maybe God has forgotten me? Maybe the transition did not go as planned and God just missed me by a hair's breadth?

Whoever, while he has been present in bodily form, has occupied himself exclusively with the *reality of the senses,* and neglected to examine the *structure of his soul,* will not be able to get around having a fear of death!

OVERCOMING FEAR OF DEATH

Throughout the course of life, everyone is confronted time and again with the processes of dying and death. Every person has countless opportunities to practice for the "final" exit, so-called death. And each person wanders through countless dying and death experiences, even though their body does not die.

When the dying and death processes can be approached

in a conscious manner with total acceptance, then actual death is simply a deeper continuation of the same.

There is the frequently expressed wish that death might come rather quickly—for example through a heart attack. Of course no one likes to put up with pain for a long time, but why does it always have to happen so fast? Is it so that I do not have to be consciously present in this time of terror? So that I don't have to look at (or be concerned with) what is going on in the hope that this makes things easier? Those are illusions.

Crossing over is easiest for those beings who have already *worked through* their associations with dying and death during their earthly lifetime. That doesn't happen mainly by soaking up scads of literature on this subject. No, it happens by consciously experiencing and working through the dying processes that continuously present themselves for practice, which do not require leaving the body, but involve relationships to our loved ones that die, conditions that we hold dear which change and therefore die, professional and sports successes that die, children that die.

There are countless dying processes that repeatedly challenge us and which confront us with the transience of every moment, every event and every structure. Whoever has reconciled himself with this transience truly in his heart (and not merely in his head), will be able to die in peace and serenity, with full consciousness.

WHAT DOES NOT WANT TO DIE?

As a rule, aspects that don't want to die are alive in every person—and even actively rebel against the dying process. The more such aspects gather together and build an alliance against dying, the more life forces are consumed in this inner battle—because this is a fight against a natural, immutable law of life. Seen from the view that I now experience, this is a waste of life energy. Why is that so?

Before entering each incarnation, every being has chosen various experiences and learning scopes. These can be experiences and learning scopes of many different sorts. Those people, who especially feel an inward pull to move around a lot and live in different places, want to experience being touched in very different facets of their own soul. If a being wants to try out these various living environments, it is an important precondition to be ready and willing to constantly let the old die at a cellular level, so that new space for new experiences is created. However, if the alliance between the death-resistant aspects continuously rebels *against* the changing structures of the environment, then being touched in the different facets of the soul cannot take place. The readiness to let events, occurrences, and circumstances die over and over again is also the main precondition for a varied, challenging, and instructive incarnation.

DEATH—TRANSFORMATION'S MOST POWERFUL FORCE

Generally speaking, the worst aspect about death to someone thinking about it is the uncertainty of what happens afterward. Death—a wide black door behind which an unknown is hiding—is usually something about which very few people want to know, or voluntarily think about. By its very nature, death inevitably presupposes that post-death life continues very differently. This viewpoint has a particular significance, because the way things continue after death eludes human control. Not only are we unaware of what is going to happen after the death of our physical body, we also don't know what is going to happen when certain aspects of our being die during an incarnation. This fact prevents us from allowing death to act as the most monumental transformer of existence, with dire consequences. Quite frequently pre-death, some aspects hang on in the death tunnel for months (if not years) and are incapable of passing through the point of death. This creates a life that Jesus so appropriately called 'tepid life'—neither truly alive nor truly dead: An unsatisfying mix that prolongs life, robs it of fun, and leads to endless conditions of illness.

If it's possible for us to really make peace with death, to see it in it's proper light, then we have given ourselves an immensely important gift—for we will have reconciled ourselves with the strongest transformer of earthly existence.

Aspects of your own being, which no longer fulfill any function, may be led into the death channel and handed over to death for their destruction. Once these aspects have passed through the point of death, the previously bound energy is once again available as new life force.

Death as a transformer has done its work and successfully fulfilled its task.

WHY DO WE RESIST DEATH?

You, dear reader, can imagine that this is a very broad and heavy subject. It is an acceptable part of society to resist death. Those people who take up arms against death are viewed both as heroes and successful. They fight and fight against death. Yet, is it a fight that can really be won? Is the fight *against* death not in truth a fight *against* oneself?

Only you alone can answer these questions. I am simply guiding you toward these important life questions. For as already noted, and as I will keep repeating: Death is not the opposite of life. Instead, death is a component of life.

If you allow yourself to be touched by these words they will gradually put death in the place it truly belongs—in the midst of life. Fighting against death uses up vast amounts of energy. And furthermore, is an uphill battle—a tough fight, a fight without end.

Most people fight against death because they have a false image of it. In the Christian teachings, still deeply impregnated in consciousness or—better said—in the collective unconscious, death is seen as a transition into the destructive trinity of hell, purgatory, and heaven. According to traditional thinking, it is decided at the time of death where, or respectively, how life will go on: For the good and obedient, heaven; for the questionably obedient, purgatory; and for those who are decidedly bad, hell.

Even when there is just the smallest inkling of such fatalistic thinking and ideas of the hereafter at work in someone, that person will fight against death—because, through death, there is the possibility of landing in hell.

The time of death is the moment when the final decision is made as to which direction the soul must take: A steep descent into hell, to the place of atonement called purgatory, or to heaven—the realm of love and peace. Do such old confused ways of thinking really invite one to die? No, of course not. It is these very images that justify the fight against death. These very images force people to keep seeing death as something that has to be fought against with every possible means and that must be delayed as long as possible.

During my entire life—or rather while I inhabited a physical body (for I am even more intensely alive since the removal of my body)—I concerned myself with the subject of death and dying. These were difficult confrontations, for whoever has thoroughly examined death rattles an old societal taboo. The taboo states, "It is better if I don't concern myself too much with the terrible bottom-line called death. It will come soon enough anyway. Rather, I will turn my attention wholeheartedly toward the luxuriant life. I will only concern myself with death when I absolutely have to."

Concerning oneself with death does not necessarily mean hanging around cemeteries and worshipping the dead. Taking an interest in death means: Placing death in its rightful place within one's own inner world, welcoming it into the orchestra of inward existence; and in the best case scenario, always having death present. For it doesn't just take things away, as is so often emphasized. Rather, it liberates by removing obstacles and energy structures that are in the way.

MY EXPERIENCES WITH DEATH

First of all, at this moment I would like to thank Bruno warmly for his willingness to translate my vibration into words: Thank you very much.

As far as dying is concerned, it would be far easier if in general the strict dividing line between the worlds were handled in a more relaxed manner, and with a lighter touch. Farewells would no longer be so radical were the communication less abruptly interrupted.

I would now like to use this opportunity to share with you, dear reader, my own personal experiences after the event of my physical death.

To begin with, death was not something I was afraid of. This was attributable to two circumstances: Having immersed myself in this subject so intensively throughout my life; and having had so many practical experiences as I accompanied other people on their respective journeys to their death.

Standing by people in their last hours was always a very intense experience for me because I would accompany them all the way to the threshold. I was able to tune in spiritually, and was allowed to go with them to the very edge of life on this side. These were heavenly experiences for me—all the more touching that I was able to make this journey from the depths of my heart over and over again.

But now it was my turn to die. I knew what it was like to leave the body, having experimented with it a lot—especially at the end of my last incarnation. However, leaving without having to return to this tight, ill-fitting garment was a completely different experience. It went much deeper, because it meant simultaneously pulling back from the Earth's field to which we are connected through the physical body by default.

Next I felt the presence of a nonmaterial being who, without words but with tremendous strength, revealed her presence and encouraged me to leave my body—because the time had now come. As previously mentioned, this occurred without speaking. It was a *knowing* transmission without words. It was simply clear. I was excited, nervous, and admittedly, also a little afraid. Accompanying others to their death is one thing; but taking this step oneself, is an altogether special and unique experience.

By allowing myself to be led out of my body and easing myself out of the Earth's energy field, images of important events from this incarnation flew past my inner eye with incredible speed; and from my soul level, I was able to sense the meaning and purpose of these past experiences. It was very profound, and moves me even now as I describe it. The many hardships, the many obstacles, and the relationship difficulties paraded by me, and at the same time, I stood right in the midst of them once again. It was as if someone had removed a picture from a billboard. And with every millimeter that was removed, another visible and audible event from my past life took place before my spiritual eye. But it wasn't merely my spiritual eye that was touched again by these experiences. It was also my heart.

The birth of my son, separating from my husband, the deep connection to my sisters, the difficult relationship with my mother, feeling rejected by my father, success in the scientific sector—all these came rushing toward me with such great force, that the simultaneous combination of their sheer amplitude and truth made me weep.

I felt alone. Yet at the same time, I felt totally held, though I could not say what caused this feeling. I was deeply touched by these experiences; and at the same time, enveloped in feelings of warmth and security. "This must be like being inside the mother's womb," I thought, as I was slowly able to remove my attention from the racing pictures of times past.

I had known about this life review from stories, although it felt very different when I experienced it for myself. What happened next, however, was previously unknown to me.

I was brought into a room brilliantly lit, with many radiant beings—an indescribably beautiful room that also felt familiar to me. I was deeply moved by this familiar place. The closer I got to these individual beings, the more familiar their energies seemed to me, until suddenly they all revealed themselves, and I found myself in the midst of faces that I knew intimately. What a reunion—indescribably touching and delightful! "Right now," I felt "I have arrived." A huge, color-delicious-feeling and reunion ensued. Those present radiated tremendous joy, and it was immediately transmitted to me. I was very touched to be back home. Most of all, I was pleased about my father's presence. Our way of relating, as it had been on Earth, was tangible again in this meeting. A great closeness and trust, yet at the same time something distant. My maternal grandmother and several cousins were also present. A celebration of unspeakable magnificence followed.

This celebration, unsurpassed in its intensity by any I had ever experienced on Earth, didn't last forever though. Soon my spirit guide led me into another room where the being sat who had accompanied me during the life I had just completed—the chief executive of my last incarnation, so to speak. I felt a great familiarity with her too, and a great respect—a respect that quite automatically and without any further thought brought me to my knees. "This is the way it really should be in church when we kneel before the Divine," I thought.

I was already being presented with my new assignment. You can imagine that I was not particularly interested in accepting new tasks. I was almost a little shocked to learn that even here new assignments would be issued and carried out.

I had preferred instead to look around and explore this new method of moving about, this new bodily feeling, and to be totally there for my loved ones. Now I was being told to go back to my body to respectfully take leave of it. That too didn't really fit in with my own ideas, but I knew that this request was right. For out of this newly won freedom, it was easy for me to go near my body and to thank it for all of its service. I also felt how a sort of attraction exuded from my physical body. From the earthly perspective, this probably all took place in only a few minutes following departure from my body; and so my body, my dear earthly cloak, was still able to receive me. Nothing, however, would change the fact that—considered from the earthly perspective—I had died. At the same time, I felt distressed that I would have to leave this body forever and ever, even though I had a long time to prepare for death, and was conscious and able to say good-bye to my body—including the mourning associated with this process.

I will never be able to hug my son again. I will never be able to let butter melt on my tongue. I will never be able to smell violets and roses and take their delicate fragrance into my body and soul. That made me sad.

I was simply sad about the fact that the existence in my human body was irrevocably over. This circumstance also seemingly separated me from the people and beings who still live in physical bodies and whom I love very much. This sadness was simply there and is present again in this moment as I share my experience. Yet the previous far-reaching experiences with my spirit-relatives and spirit-siblings allowed my sadness to dissipate in an instant. A great joy overcame me in the knowledge that I could be united with many deeply loved beings. So I gave my body a spiritual candle and a bough of evergreen with the purpose of assisting its dissolution.

In this way I was able to say good-bye to my body in peace and with joy—at least initially. For the process of leaving the physical body happens suddenly through the finer structured bodies emerging all at once from the physical body. However, on the psychological level, it takes more time to completely detach from the physical body.

There are beings that are barely able to make this separation. They want vehemently to go back into their body. These are beings who, during their earthly existence, suffered greatly from an inability to let go.

I then started once again on my path to my master—the one in whose presence I automatically sank to my knees. We discussed a few details about the incarnation I had just left behind. But above all, we discussed the task upon which I was now to embark in the finer-structured world. As mentioned before, there was a part of me that wasn't at all ready to take on new tasks so soon—in part because I hadn't expected it.

My master spoke very lovingly to me—so lovingly and with her eyes shining so brightly, I had to believe everything she told me. She drew me completely into her sphere with her energy, so that the idea never entered my mind that she might make a request of me that I would be unable to fulfill.

She spoke thus; "Dear Elisabeth, during your time on Earth, you have been intensely busy with death, dying and their transitions. Because you were so courageous and unafraid to speak about these taboos in human society, you enabled many people to make this transition in a relaxed and even joyful manner. And your work does not end because you left your physical body behind. Your work continues and I would prefer to call it a *service of love*—as "work" still carries the vibration of "must" or "duty." Service of love, on the other hand, expresses a correspondence with what you want to do: Serve your dear ones with love."

So spoke my master. And I saw endless love streaming forth from her heart while she was speaking. It seemed to me as though she were simply speaking out of my innermost being. And that felt so deep and good. I had the feeling that my innermost self had manifested in the form in which she appeared to me, and was speaking to me in this way. I was filled with light and the deep feeling of having arrived. Quite simply, it felt heavenly.

She spoke further, "The work that you have done on Earth has shed light on the subject of dying to many people. And that is how your service of love will continue now: On the one hand, by teaching beings who are preparing to incarnate about the subjects of death, abandonment and loneliness; on the other hand, you will spread knowledge gained by the real experience of your transition to the hereafter through human beings who have the ability and gift to perceive such communications. For now, these are the two main elements upon which you may embark in your service of love. Furthermore, you will have plenty of time left for playing, dancing, and joyful togetherness with your beloved spirit siblings. There are lots of stories you will be allowed to share. But, as I explained to you, the service of love is of great importance and therefore has first priority."

And as you see, here I am—fulfilling my service of love!

For Bruno, it is a great challenge right now to allow me to work through him without intervening in this process with his own being. And I have the task of transmitting these truths—through his body—while at the same time respecting his sovereignty over this body. That means that I do not simply take over his whole body, but rather that I agree not to overly strain his spiritual channel which he offers for my use. The agreement is that he decides when the connection is open for me to use it, and when it isn't. I can tell you, this is quite a challenge for me. During my lifetime, I could take my typewriter whenever I wanted, and just hammer away. In this collaboration with Bruno, I always have to wait until the channel is open; be alert to whenever his many duties leave a little of his capacity in reserve; and furthermore, wait until it is not too noisy in his house for the energy transmission to take place.

Good. This is just an aside, so the reader can get a sense of the practical side of this work with regard to what it takes for this book to come about.

Now let's get on with our service of love. I can offer you no concept of how you should die, nor what to do, and what not to do. That would not serve matters discussed here at all. I can only help you focus on the essential points, so that before and during the dying process you will not, to the best of your ability, be overcome with paralyzing fear as a consequence of ignoring and postponing the subject during your lifetime.

THE DISPOSABLE MENTALITY

There is frequent talk of a disposable society. This society lives under the motto: "Whatever I can't use anymore, I will dispose of." Things that no longer work end up in the landfill without so much as a second thought. Is death then also about eliminating that which doesn't function properly anymore? Is the disposable society a result of a mindless overachieving principle? Or is the disposable society in perfect harmony with death since death helps us to dispose of that which is no longer needed? I assert that the disposable society is based on the fear of death.

It isn't about immediately eliminating that which is no longer functional; but instead it has to do with accompanying it appropriately to its death. If I use this principle in regard to material goods, then when an object is no longer fulfilling its purpose, I can thank it for its service and dispose of it appropriately. It is then not being thrown away, but instead respectfully handed over to death for transformation.

At this point, it is worth stating once again that death does not cause extinction. It is a transformation of energy. If this basic principle is not recognized, then death will continue to be connected to fear in every case.

Therefore, it is not about death having an effect. It is about how I handle the effects of death. If I am successful in recognizing death as an important entity of life, then a new way of handling this principle arises. The aspects that move through the dying process until they reach death may be escorted in a dignified and appropriate manner rather than entertaining the attitude "death exists, but I ignore it."

In this context, an aspect is accompanied to death rather than disposed of. Moreover when this accompaniment is implemented with emotional participation—with presence—then, in a natural way, space for something new arises.

It is very enlightening to note that through the production of atomic electricity—a very potent power—a waste product is created that cannot be disposed of for thousands of years. This does not occur in nature. When a society has difficulty eliminating waste on such a massive scale, then that is also a picture of its disturbed relationship to death.

DENIAL OF THE DEATH PRINCIPLE

The death principle can be avoided in many different ways—for example, by continuously producing new things without disposing of the old ones in an appropriate way, or without dissolving emotional connections to old ones. In order to avoid facing the transitory nature of old things, this is evident in the constant search for (and consumption of) new things. In relationships, this phenomenon can appear as an inclination to change partners frequently, without working through the previous relationship. The result are landfills for which no one wants to be responsible. Whereupon among political parties, the responsibility is unkindly shifted and blame is gladly distributed.

In order for us to take full responsibility for our existence, our life, and our choice to be here on Earth, we must first be capable of appropriately disposing of various aspects of our existence. If we are incapable of this, we will always carry 'waste' within, gladly shifting the responsibility to others. Parents, teachers, and the government are prevalent screens on which we project those aspects of ourselves we either don't know how to handle, dispose of, or for which we don't assume responsibility.

In this way we come back to the question "how can I allow the unresolved within myself to die?"

HOW DO I LET UNRESOLVED ISSUES DIE?

As a rule, there are two ways to deal with a problem: Either do something to resolve the problem, or do nothing and push it away in the hope that it will resolve itself in time. To these two principles of doing and not doing (active and passive), I would like to add a third principle which is located at the level of existence—the principle of dying. Some say dying belongs to the passive principle. With dying, I don't have to contribute anything. But that is definitely not the case. Dying has nothing to do with general passivity. In truth, dying has everything to do with activity. By that is meant activity at the right time and in the right place, and passivity at the right time and in the right place. That is the high art of dying.

Perhaps a better understanding can be imparted when looked at in this way: Similar to the successful nutritional absorption of food whereby the esophagus remains open when food passes to the stomach, it is equally important on the psychological level that the death canal is ready for the transformation process. This basic readiness comes about primarily through the recognition of what death truly is. If one assumes that death is a great enemy who could possibly deceive and undermine life, then this attitude will also show up in the death canal. Tension is the result. Tension in the death canal causes delays and an increased occurrence of complications. And as a result, dying becomes a painful and unsatisfying process.

If the aspect that now needs to go through death's door meets an elastic and flexible death canal, then the death of this aspect can happen in as little as three minutes, and transformation is complete!

During such successful transformational experiences arises a feeling that dying—even if sometimes painful and connected to strong emotions—is and does good; and in the long term, brings joyful changes.

It is about the experience that—out of dying—rather than nothing, something *new* arises.

THE ATTITUDE TOWARD DEATH IS SIGNIFICANT

Take some time to scrutinize your own attitude toward death. More than you realize is connected to it.

Occurrences in your life have much more to do with

your attitude toward death than you think. For this reason, it really makes a lot of sense to become aware of your attitude toward death.

Please take a few moments and ask to come into contact with the energy of death within you. Feel it and take your time, lay this book aside for a little while, and then, in your own time, allow the next few sections to have an effect on you.

- What does the word death trigger in me? Does it compress my energy field, or can I be present with the flow of breath and the flow of bodily sensations while I think about death?

- Is death (and contact with it) neutral for me, or is it something that has an immediate effect on me?

- Does the word death bring a feeling of fear, or repulsiveness, or something I really want to avoid completely?

- Can I also imagine that death can bring about something joyful, or is death just the destroyer, the annihilator, the one that extinguishes everything?

Let these questions resound through you a few times. Simply let them sink in and observe within yourself what you perceive without judgment. You now have the opportunity to get a little closer to yourself, because by observing your ideas about death, it becomes possible for you to come into contact with yourself on a deeper level.

DIALOGUE BETWEEN ELISABETH & BRUNO PART I

E: Now, dear Bruno, you have already examined death quite extensively. What does death mean to you?

B: For me, seen from a distance, death is something neutral. The idea of leaving my body behind is a very distant prospect for me right now. On the other hand, I have already been working very intensely at allowing dying processes within myself for a long time. I have also been accompanying character aspects to their death; and in that regard, I am quite familiar with it.

E: Are you afraid of death?

B: No, I am not afraid of death—which doesn't mean that I will die without any problems or without any difficulty. In the course of my spiritual path, I have been confronted with death on a very deep level. It was about parts of the ego that had to die and go through death's gate. Aspects of the ego—which I didn't recognize at first as such—came up again and again, and subsequently led me into very painful situations. And because I am not especially eager to experience painful situations, it is very important to me to lead these ego-aspects through the dying process into their death. Because the ego largely consists of pain, it is my view that by enabling the ego (the pain) to surface it can subsequently be allowed to heal through the death process.

E: You expressed it beautifully. Many people are afraid of the pain caused by death. Yet, at the same time, they lose sight of the fact of how much pain death is capable of removing. This is significant, because through this insight, ideas regarding death change on a fundamental level, thereby establishing a true relationship with death rather than one dominated by fearful images.

Why do you think we are writing this book together? Do you have any idea?

B: Oh yes, I do. Before we began this book project a few weeks ago, an intense dying process was taking place within me. I had the feeling of having come to the bottom of my existence in this life. I found things there that were deeply life-inhibiting to me. Again and again, aspects, influences and experiences from old times would come up, and I had the feeling they no longer belonged to me. During this time, I came into very intense contact with death. In my youth, this expressed itself in the form of suicidal thoughts. In this latest process, I was able to experience how healing it is *ON A FULLY CONSCIOUS LEVEL* to allow aspects of the personality to die that are often connected to fear.

Not easy work. But as I said, very healing and eventually very freeing.

E: Would you say that you have reconciled yourself with death?

B: Whether or not it is a complete reconciliation, I cannot say. Often it is so that, on a spiritual path, new and surprising moments happen over and over—that parts of me are brought into my consciousness that I had never even dreamed existed within my being. That is why I cannot answer this question conclusively. What I can definitely say is that the old image of the Grim Reaper no longer has any effect on me. The belief in being totally extinguished has never really made me afraid.

Also, I was never afraid of that during my entire incarnation because on a soul level I simply knew that this is not real. However, it has to be said that during puberty (or even later) I wouldn't have minded being completely wiped out—due to lack of direction, inability to grasp the meaning of painful conditions, or being overwhelmed.

E: That sounds almost a little dramatic!

B: Why?

E: The aspect of being completely wiped out.

B: Didn't you ever have any such feelings during the time you were incarnated?

E: No, I wanted to live with every fiber of my being. In addition to that, when I was exploring death, it wasn't just on an emotional level, it was also on a scientific level. At the time, that gave me a healthy distance from the whole subject. I believe that in this regard you are more of a feeling-type person.

B: Yes, that is absolutely right. I have to be—including for work like this. Otherwise, you wouldn't be able to channel your energy through my field so easily.

E: What about the theme of death in your family of origin? Can you perceive any tendencies?

B: Yes, there is certainly also fear of dying present; but

from my point of view, it has been largely worked through.

E: Your grandfather is here now and he would like to say a few words about that. Is that all right with you?

B: Today is the kind of day that requires my flexibility. It takes so much effort to switch back and forth so fast, but I wouldn't dream of not welcoming my dear grandfather. My ears are already burning.

G: My warmest greetings to you, my dear Grandson. As it happens, it is easier for me to answer these questions from the spiritual level about how the family dynamics in which you operate handle death. First of all, there is certainly considerable suppression. The deep Catholic structures that I too bravely carried during my incarnation, have contributed a lot to how death was kept secret as much as possible. At the same time, through a very deep heart connection and emotional sensitivity, there was fear that death would separate the beloved family structure. We didn't make much room for death. But when someone died, we were deeply touched by it.

B: Yes, I know this phenomenon too. Whenever someone died, I would always react with contemplation, inwardness, and with growing calm. It often got on my nerves when other people quickly dismissed the event and turned their attention to something else. I felt that this did not offer the due respect to the loss and to the departed.

G: Yes, this turning inward is part of our family structure, which is all right as it is. But it seems important to me that this structure is mentioned and recognized. So, I now leave the field to Elisabeth again.

B: Thank you very much for your visit.

E: I would have loved such a Grandfather. The way he so strongly stands by the whole family from the spirit realm, he is almost constantly helping and supporting all of you!

Good, let's go back to our core topic. Do you have the feeling that when the time is ripe for you to make the final crossing into the spirit world, you will be able to handle it in a relaxed manner?

B: You really ask very direct questions!

Yes, I do have this feeling—although it will probably be difficult for me to leave my current wonderful family situation. But that is the way I see things right now.

Through meditation and other experiences where my nonphysical bodies separated from my physical body and were able to move around freely, I've already experienced letting go of some of the nonmaterial parts of my being. Conclusion: I am definitely not afraid of changing planes. Quite the opposite: I imagine that to be quite an adventure. However, I imagine the separation from my loved ones, as a result of no longer living in a physical body, will be very bitter.

E: In that regard, I would like to tell you a little from my wealth of experiences:

Interestingly enough, I am now closer to those people whom I loved very much, and who still live in a body. The multitude of images and ideas that have such a strong divisive function on the earthly plane, no longer have that effect on me on the spiritual plane, as they did during my incarnation. That means, I can for example think myself into my son's heart, and I am immediately present there. Present in a feeling sense. That was (and is) a very strong experience. Even when I do not enter the thoughts or feelings of that relevant person (there is such a thing as a personality protection, even on this level), I am totally connected with the person on a soul and heart level. This means what you are afraid of is only partially correct. Of course, giving someone a hug is something else entirely when the person that I spiritually hug has no idea that he is being hugged—or just doesn't believe in this nonmaterial reality.

Furthermore, the sensation is very different without a body: lighter, freer, and more relaxed, because the whole burden of existence is not weighing us down. For, on my current level of existence, we definitely do not have to worry about salary, paying bills, getting food, having children, physical pain and illness and the corresponding healing methods that go with it. We can leave that confidently to the Earth inhabitants. Honestly, I don't miss that either.

Can you imagine that separation doesn't have to be so painful?

B: Yes, I can imagine that. But jumping around on the trampoline with my daughter and having such great fun; or joyfully munching on freshly baked bread—that will definitely be over.

E: It is so that humans and spirit beings are often together on a developmental path. Many times the human being only realizes some small part of this. In such a case, the spirit being takes part in the sensory impressions of that particular person. The presence of the spirit being gives the person the impression of being aware of something more extensively than usual—a form of expanded consciousness. Both the spirit being and the human being benefit from this mutual encounter. That is the highest form of a win/win situation—when the spirit being and the human being are allowed to meet each other in an extensive sensory-based encounter. People who are aware of, and have made an inner decision to be open to the spiritual world are constantly accompanied and touched by spirit beings and spirit guides. That doesn't necessarily make their existence easier, but it certainly does make it richer and fuller.

B: What is this like for you, this separation that is maintained by us (i.e., people) between this world and the hereafter, and that in my experience also seems to have a particular function?

E: This separation does not exist for me. It is, as you have correctly ascertained, a product from "your side" which, with regard to its development thus far, did once have a function. However, many columns of light are increasingly perforating this separation.

The wall is beginning to crumble. It is a process that takes time. But I do hope that the wall's destruction doesn't take as long as its construction—which required many thousands of years. Now there are gateways. As mentioned earlier, this separation does not exist for us on the spiritual side. It can simply be that we don't especially enjoy, or desire, penetrating the denseness—particularly the denseness of thought of earth's inhabitants. Indeed, that sometimes requires a concerted effort to penetrate the heart of a human being behind their self-erected walls.

I am still working on aligning my consciousness with

the new structures of this level because the return to the spiritual world does not automatically make everything different. In the spiritual world, I have to integrate aspects of my soul step by step again. I am constantly discovering new parts that surface into my consciousness—parts of my soul that were not incarnated in the earthly structure. For this reason, I am still finding my way on the other side. Can you comprehend that?

B: Yes, I can understand that very well. I am familiar with the fact that the whole soul does not incarnate into a human being, but only the aspects that want to be further developed in Earth's school. At first I was afraid of this thought, or knowledge. In the meantime, I find it pleasant that who I am here is not all that I am. That gives me hope there will be beautiful reunions with parts of myself that were left behind. In addition, I find that I have plenty of material here for further development.

E: Yes, indeed there are people who are full of characteristics they want to further develop. Often these are people who have difficult biographies such as setbacks, complex relationships, demanding professional challenges, and so on.

In this regard, you have taken on quite a lot, and it looks like (between you and me) you are well on your way to reaching your soul's goal.

B: Are there people who don't reach their life goals?

E: There are beings whose plans are so great that it is certainly possible they will add another incarnation in order to accomplish all they aspire to.

Mainly, I want to say that, in the end, something like dying does not even exist. To be able to recognize that, you must solidly get to know death and play with it, without any tricks or twists, in order to know that life does indeed go on after dying—and especially after death.

DEATH IS DIFFERENT FROM OUR PERCEPTION OF IT

As previously mentioned, death is the strongest transformative power of all. The question is: Why is it so significant to actualize transformation?

Transformation is death's little sister. It has similar characteristics, but is not as radical as death.

Transformation is the process that allows the vibrational frequency to be raised in the midst of the denseness of incarnated existence. To transform something means to bring a substance into a new form. Why is that so important right at this time?

There were times, and I am now speaking mainly of the dark Middle Ages, that were not about transformation.

At that time, it was more about humans experiencing what happens when vibrational frequencies are lowered. Having to constantly stay in the same situation, to constantly be at the mercy of the same passions, to constantly be caught in the same old patterns; as seen from a spiritual perspective, this sort of standstill—and the resulting injuries—were signatures of the Middle Ages.

But the here and now is about totally different intentions. Prior to their birth, people who are currently incarnated felt attracted by the enormous changes, interesting possibilities, and deep upheaval taking place at this moment. The world finds itself in a current comparable to the beginning of civilization in America: Much is possible, open, and depends on the strength of individuals, and what they are able to accomplish. Adventurers, inventors, and creative people are needed. Whoever relies solely on tradition and has no courage to take risks won't get far in these times.

The spirit world is sending immense amounts of energy into the Earth structure and its field; and, figuratively speaking, is continuously breathing the word *TRANS-FORMATION* into the energies that have been sent. Everything is being remodeled. That doesn't make things any easier; but, on balance in today's day and age, there can be no talk of boredom. Departure, letting go of the old, watching out that your feet don't get pulled out from under you in the midst of this super-fast development—all of these are important aspects of the current developmental phase.

Where does death now stand in this picture of tremendous change and lightning-fast development? What significance is attributed to death?

Death has the function of accommodation at this time. The energy of death cleans up, gets rid of things, and thereby makes space for that which is new. Old useless structures that many years ago were a blessing for all mankind are now in the way and must be demolished so that new structures can be built on a good foundation. Therefore, it is very beneficial for all development if fear and death can be separated from their often narrow and destructive embrace, and disabled from preventing profound renewals.

This is not about breaking with mankind's history, or about blaming it. Every so often the traditions and experiences of the past may be called upon for advice. But because the changes are so fundamental, and are happening at such high velocity, the answers to many of the questions are rarely to be found in the past. Rather, they are to be found in the creativity of now, which cannot be solved with the philosophical ideas from our Grandfathers' time. Rather a dynamic confrontation and clear vision are what is needed at this time.

A further relevant point is the direct communication with the spiritual world. In just a few decades, it will become quite a natural part of the western world—so that things may be planned and developed together consciously. Spiritual beings are often the visitors of the Earth's sphere of tomorrow! In this regard, a continual interaction takes place. Additionally, the spiritual world has access to an incredible potential of creativity and strength because the absence of the fight for existence doesn't unnecessarily use up energy.

The strict separation between this side and the hereafter is with absolute certainty a boundary consecrated to death. At the beginning, there are pioneers who are preparing the changes for the masses—and now that means only a few are able to cross this boundary.

At a later time, the contact with guardian angels, dear friends, and previous relatives who are in the spiritual world; and, in the best case scenario, contact with inner guidance—one's own inner core—will be nurtured and cared for without much ado.

DEATH OF THE PERSONALITY

This form of death is always available to us. We always have the choice of letting our personality die.

From this earthly point of view, it is about building the personality, stabilizing it, and expressing it. Viewed from the spiritual dimension, the personality is something that stands in the way of contacting the original principle of creation. One's own personality is bound to the ego. "I am different" is the main motto of the separated personalities. "No one is like me." These are qualities rooted in the ego. I don't want to generalize and make the ego sound bad or devilish. Not at all. The fact is, the ego solidly and unwaveringly gets in the way of much that human beings desire to be.

Who then does the ego get in the way of? The ego is the part of me that helps me become something in the world. The ego makes sure I am not a doormat—that I don't give up. The ego fights. The ego does everything to achieve improvements. The ego engages on its own behalf!

If a person intends to let go of separation and come into ONENESS, then it is clear: The ego needs to be sacrificed. ONENESS and EGO do not get along very well for the simple reason that the ego is a result of separation from the Divine.

To dissolve the separation, the result (ego) has to be removed, or at least reduced, to an absolute minimum. Few people are able to let go of their ego all at once. Usually there is such a strong identification with the ego that its dying brings up the fear that the person might also die. This is what prevents the human being from letting go of his ego. This is why the death of the ego is not very widespread. Besides, it is a long process—a dying process of many layers that repeatedly require an inner decision, and the corresponding readiness to let go in depth. However, once someone has made the decision (in agreement with his soul) to let his ego die, then as a rule there is no turning back.

DIALOGUE BETWEEN ELISABETH & BRUNO—PART II

E: You assume that you will be able to die without any major problems, and that only the separation from your family would create any pain for you. Are you still of this opinion?

B: I assume that leaving the body is both a loss and liberation.

E: I don't have to travel for two or four hours to get to someone who is close to me. I can, through thought, connect myself with the field of that person and journey in this way to her. Once I am present with this person, I can take part in her thoughts, her feelings, maybe even taste the delicious cookie that she is wolfing down in ravenous hunger.

Once I have had enough of this reality, then I am free to just zip away. I visit my beloved friends from my earthly incarnation over and over. While their bodies are asleep, their energy bodies travel around, and we meet and share wonderful moments with each other, and then I accompany them back to their bodies. That person usually remembers little or nothing of our encounters.

B: Do you not suffer when the people you visit don't realize that you are present?

E: In the beginning that was very painful for me, when I realized that my loved ones were not reacting to me in their usual way. I no longer felt pained once I realized that I am now able to touch them much more deeply on a soul level than I could when I was embodied on Earth. With a few of my dear ones, I maintain heart to heart conversations, which is enormous fun.

Since my "passing over" I feel much stronger, and have the feeling that I can actually make more of the things happen that I want to accomplish. I don't experience any resistance from the material world, and that gives me a great feeling of satisfaction.

B: You mean, I should be happily awaiting the hereafter?

E: Above all, I recommend that you fully and wholeheartedly be exactly where you are right now. For in the end, it doesn't matter where you are. It is secondary whether you live in China or in Switzerland. What is important is the quality of your awareness, wherever you are in this moment. Comparison is not the issue. The issue is being completely present wherever you are. And if a person is fully present in the here-and-now, then he has an opening for the world of spirit. People are less reachable from the spiritual world when they continually live in the past or in the future, and not where they belong—in the present.

B: I have the feeling that being present now opens doors that otherwise would remain closed. I often had the experience though that—through the presence of the spiritual world—I got pulled into the future.

E: What do you mean?

B: By opening myself to the nonmaterial levels, I was able to perceive prophecies or pointers regarding the future. In the meantime, I respond with apprehension to such information, because I find that the future provides an abundant ground for projections.

E: Know that the spirit world can blow up existing wishes and ideas for greater clarity. That can only happen when a certain affinity exists within you for these wishes and ideas. This is a blessing, because it mirrors back to you what is already inside you. This law of "mirroring" can be applied to human-to-human relationships, as well as to human-to-spirit relationships. That is why it is so important that humans who come into contact with the spiritual world are well grounded within themselves. Otherwise, the type of dramas that are present between humans could continue to be acted out in the relationships between humans and spirits—and that is something we obviously do not want.

B: No, certainly not.

E: You can assume that if you receive prophecies from the spiritual world, then either unresolved aspects of yourself are being worked out (exaggerated), or wishes that you may have are vibrating in the spiritual realm and are being reflected back to you as prophecies. In this respect, the future is an excellent field for projections; and it always makes sense when projections die. When confronted with reality, projections prefer to die.

INTEGRATING DEATH INTO LIFE

As mentioned before, death is not the opposite of life; instead it is a component of life. That should have become clear through the course of this book. Let's go a step farther and ask ourselves: What is life really? Is it a succession of joyful and sorrowful situations, events, and coincidences, or is it more? If man is keen to enjoy life to the exclusion of death, then it is indeed so—that life is a succession of positive and negative events. If, however, death is successfully integrated into life, then the polarity is eliminated and life does not split into comfortable, positive, and lively, versus uncomfortable, negative, and moribund.

Through the integration of death, it even becomes possible to enjoy the dying process, and to know that a process is taking place that creates room for something new. This is equally applied to the dying of aspects of one's own personality, as well as to the death of the body.

Actually, the nonmaterial being who leaves the body upon death is only one aspect of a greater whole. For in a person, only parts of the soul are incarnated at one time.

Therefore, the issue around dying is not just about an excarnation[7] process, it is also about a new incarnation into the spiritual world.

EXPERIENCES WITH
THE EX- & INCARNATION PROCESSES

By leaving my body (the excarnation process), I not only distanced myself from the earthly plane, I stepped into a new realm, in which I was the same as I was in the earthly dimension; but—and this is essential—I was much, much more. As I was leaving my body, I had begun to suspect that I was more than I had assumed during my "lifetime." It is somewhat like when a child finds himself continually confronted with new aspects of his personality as he is growing up. Here, in the spiritual world, I often had that experience: Aha, this is me, too; yes, great; and this too is me as well. Constantly, new dimensions of my being are joining me that I had forgotten were (parts of) me too. These are very comprehensive experiences that are not so easy to put into words. It is as if one could dive into a whole new volume about oneself, and almost not understand how one could have forgotten that this is also a component of oneself.

Beings who have difficulty letting go of earthly reality, prevent the process of recognizing who and what they really are. One of my tasks is to accompany beings in that process and encourage them to let go of the Earth, so that they can accept the gift of expanded existence altogether.

Humanity is now also involved in this process—being called to dissolve the bonds with conservative, narrow-minded ideas, so that the more comprehensive version of one's true being can find its place and manifest.

For if you knew how much more you are than you imagine yourselves to be, you would be doing cartwheels. For many beings who now find themselves on the earthly plane, this is a very important task: To manifest the wider version of their highest self into the earthly realm. I want to emphasize that the body is fully capable of hosting that broader inner being. It is a fairy tale to believe that the earthly body is too dense to integrate and manifest the broader, more comprehensive higher self. The body is a highly flexible medium that most certainly is not averse to the reality of a higher vibration. What does make it more difficult to integrate the higher vibrating reality into the body is that the body is usually beset with so many old structures, that there is hardly any room available to take in the new. And so we have circled back to our favorite main subject: Death. It is the great expander. It is able to free the depths of human existence. It is the all-encompassing and important "clear" button that brings everything back to zero.

WHO IS RESPONSIBLE FOR MY DEATH?

Have you ever asked yourself this question? Who actually determines the time of my death? Are there special circumstances that cause the demise? For example, if I am not careful enough when I am cleaning the windows, I fall off the chair, hit my head, and die,—is it coincidental, the confluence of different factors, or is there more to it?

The time of death is a dynamic affair. It is not engraved anywhere in God's Book when someone is going to return to the spiritual world. Rather, it is a question of development. Are there enough opportunities for this particular human being to develop himself in the current surroundings? Are the tasks that the soul set for itself in this incarnation completed? Is the body still in a corresponding condition to be able to master the desired learning? Does the person find himself in conditions that serve his development? (The circumstances that best serve development are not always comfortable ones.)

These and many other factors play a considerable role regarding the time of death. Usually a person does not have to consider the task of determining the timing of his death. It is his inner guidance (higher self) that is responsible for this decision. More highly developed beings, who have merged with their guidance, often determine the time of their death themselves, simply for the reason that (in their consciousness) they are no longer separated from their higher self. As a result, they are who determine their time of death.

Part II

DEATH IS A COMPONENT OF LIFE –NOT ITS OPPOSITE.

HOW DEATH IS SEPARATED FROM LIFE

Every incarnation begins with birth. As a rule, it is a joyful event when the mother and father can give the newly arrived soul space—both inwardly and outwardly. Birth is thus a joyful celebration. In the parts of the world where I lived, dying and death were a sorrowful spectacle. Why is that so? It could be the other way around. Birth could be a sorrowful spectacle, and death could be a joyful celebration. "With all my heart, I congratulate him on getting through all the intense years of schooling, and now being able to return to the spiritual world." That's what it could sound like in a few years. But until that time, there is still quite a lot of work to be done. Many images and obstacles concerning death must be led through the "death canal" in order to undergo a profound transformation. This transformation would then allow someone to depart his incarnation in the receptive manner described above.

I will now offer you a few memorable statements for you to absorb and allow to resonate from within. Are you ready to shake up some taboo zones in the collective unconscious a little within yourself? Good. Then let's begin:

1. Death is a human construct, of which one is no longer in control.

2. Death as a human construct separates us from the universe.

3. Within this separate construct, the human being perceives having been abandoned by God, and thus experiences suffering.

4. This construct of death allows humans the possibility of experiencing a Godless existence.

5. The construct of death forces the human being to experience himself as separate from God.

6. The human being now believes in the reality of death, including its boundaries—just as zoo animals no longer recall their original homes, but rather the parameters of their cages.

7. The human being redeems death only by seeing through it—and its impact—with love.

8. Contact with the spiritual world is a way to begin dissolving this destructive border.

9. Death finds its redemption in God, if the human being lets go.

10. Everything is in God, even death.

It may be that your ability to grasp these statements has your hair standing on end. However, your soul knows of what I am speaking. If you allow your soul to be touched by these statements, something will most definitely happen from within. But if these words are stopped by rationale—as is often the case—they won't make any sense.

THE WALLS OF RATIONALITY

Humankind has a very long history of suffering impregnated in our cellular memory that always accompanies us. The ego wishes whenever possible to prevent suffering. But the ego is also a product of suffering due to being separated from God. Therefore it cannot be left to the ego to interrupt suffering.

The product of suffering (ego) cannot get to the root of suffering. Rationality is very closely connected to the ego; together they keep making plans to abandon the merry-go-round of suffering. Unfortunately, this collaboration is not viable in order to redeem suffering because it's impossible for the *result* to heal the *cause*. In addition, the emphasis on rationality is a result of soul injury. *Only the act of coming into contact with the cause of suffering is capable of healing it.* The cause for all suffering lies in the fact that the soul decided to have the experience of being separated from God. The walls of rationality are a result of God-separation. It is that simple.

As a result, it would be good for humans to let the walls of rationality crumble in order to allow the soul to be touched.

DEATH & REBIRTH

If we view these numerous incarnations as a chapter in a book, and the book as the content of the soul's experiences, than we will be able to see that the book is certainly the summary of all those experiences, but that it is not the soul itself. The soul, in the depth of its being, knows that death does not exist—even though it desired the experience of death.

Death partitions the various chapters of the soul's development. What a burden it would be to have to live the whole book at once! For many beings, it is a blessing that this line of separation (bodily death) happens between these chapters. Just imagine how strenuous it would be to live for a thousand or more years in one body. Every being deserves a break. Yet now the procedure of reincarnation is gradually transformed. The separation between now and the hereafter (which so far has been almost impenetrable) is becoming more and more blurred, and will eventually be completely dissolved. The age of separation is over. Long live unity within and without! Long live the removal of separation between now and the hereafter.

From the sound of eternity (which is at the bottom of every soul) humans increasingly experience death as simply an aid and nothing more. The deeper a person penetrates into the structure of his soul (by overcoming reason), the more the spectre of death disintegrates, and the more fragile the separation between the individual chapters (lifetimes) becomes. The lines of separation between the individual chapters should no longer be considered uncrossable. On the contrary, it becomes more and more possible for the human being to consider individual chapters (incarnations) from the perspective of his soul. He can thereby harvest the gold (insights from individual incarnations) and release the details of experience and sufferings of those incarnations.

ALLOWING DEATH TO DIE

At some time or other, the soul is called to let death die as a line of demarcation between incarnations. And that is what is meant by immortality. At some point, death will have fulfilled its purpose, and it too will need to be accompanied through the death canal. This is the task awaiting us all, and that Jesus before us lived in such an exemplary way. Through his death, he overcame death. That is the soul's most difficult task. In the meantime, during each cycle of incarnation, death has become a massive criminal. In this final task, the culprit must first be loved, and then extinguished by its own hand. In this manner, immortality doesn't become some vague faraway concept; rather, it becomes an experienced reality. People who have contacted the spark of immortality within themselves can complete their last incarnation without any type of fear, and proceed joyfully at last through the earthly door of death.

JESUS CHRIST & DEATH

Jesus Christ represents the perfect union of the human being with the spirit of Christ. The human Jesus is totally risen in the Christ consciousness. His life also shows what is going to happen to each of us sooner or later: Reunion with the spirit of God. Through the unification of Jesus with the Christ light, a gateway (a developmental path), was formed that can be utilized by every human being.

Jesus simply reminded us that it is possible; and, through his example, demonstrated how he accomplished this transition—this new merger. But the question remains, are we interested enough to take on this arduous path? Jesus only showed us what is possible for all of us: Overcoming death.

Death is not conquered through technical aids or the latest modern technology. Instead, it is overcome when humans sift through their layers of conditioning, their ego structures that have been collecting throughout their many incarnations, and the delusions that they themselves have constructed over centuries—in order to recognize who they truly are.

DEATH & TRANSFORMATION

As we have already heard many times, death is most often misunderstood. And in society, death is always seen as being out of place. Therefore, a new culture for death needs to be developed: A death culture that integrates death, and appreciates it as a great life transformer.

Medicine fights full force against death. Doctors, by the nature of their profession, are obligated to conquer illness and delay death. This as such cannot really be criticized too harshly. However, today's life prolonging techniques are utilized with such intensity, and survival is fraught with such fervent fierceness, that absurd forms have developed out of it: Motionless bodies vegetating in hospital beds, forced by machines to breathe mechanically, and much worse. As previously mentioned, there is nothing to contradict the view "to maintain life at all costs." The point is that the actual problem begins when the fear of death becomes the motivating force for these measures. Then the motivation is mixed up with "unhealthy death." Unhealthy death is a death infected with fear, which therefore cannot have a natural effect. This form of death in a pact with fear works exceedingly slowly! Death that cannot freely perform its task, and fulfill its mission of transformation, is thereby crippled— a death debilitated by fear.

A death that can simply just happen, that can have an effect, is connected to true life.

TRUE LIFE

Is true life then a life in which death does not exist?

Is true life only present when death is overcome?

Can death even be overcome?

True life integrates death and does not exclude it. Death finds redemption when it does not have to be fought against—when it is seen as the blessing it truly is.

When a person can put himself trustingly in the hands of death, when he can align with death in friendship (and perhaps even gratitude) for the process of transformation that death allows him to undergo, then death is truly integrated with life.

When fear (in conjunction with death) is only first examined on the deathbed, it is often too late. Those people who are fear based and incapable of letting go, get swept into the spiritual world through death. They missed the opportunity during their lifetime to confront death. They searched for what appeared to be true life in numerous activities, self-avoidance, and from within society—rather than themselves.

TRUE LIFE & DEATH BELONG TOGETHER

You are now probably asking yourself what true life really is anyway? Is there such a thing as a false life?

Yes, there is. There is a life that is not founded in truth. A life built on illusion that motivates the human being through deception. One such deception is the unconscious attempt to escape death. How many people have tried to engrave themselves on the memory of humankind by performing heroic deeds or committing indescribable crimes? It is a motivation that originates from fear of the finality of death. In this sense, because I doubt my immortality, I will do everything in my power to leave a lasting impression on people in order to obtain a shred of immortality. Countless deeds are driven by this motivation. It is a mighty power.

How would the world look now if these people had not been driven by the motivation to immortalize themselves? And would mankind be on a less developed technical level if the spirit of invention had not been driven by this self same motivation?

Certainly, what can be said is this: Because wanting to be good at something is so closely linked to the fear of death, competition between people pollutes the path.

Do you believe this? Does it seem a little far-fetched to you? Let's take a closer look at the connection between the fear of death and the fight for competition:

We have now discovered that the fear of death is very deeply embedded in the subconsciousness of humanity—and is in fact not much younger than humanity itself. Through separation from God, humans segregated themselves almost imperceptibly from the knowledge that that which exists in God-consciousness would never dream of the idea of being extinguished forever and ever. This idea can only thrive in the fertile soil of an already present distance from divine consciousness. Once distanced from divine consciousness, death received more and more power. That power was subsequently experienced as the supreme authority, completely capable of extinguishing life—an incredible power attributable to death. The more this image of being eradicated forever took effect, the more human beings tried to erect an opposing reality. This opposing reality looks like this:

It is centrally important for me to be acknowledged and seen by my fellow men. Only then do I feel alive.
In order to be seen and acknowledged, I must either be extremely good or extremely bad, violent, or completely oppositional to societal norms.
These opposing realities cause enormous competition. For the ground rule says: I must be better than others in

order to escape final extinction.

For this reason, I maintain that competition is motivated by an unconscious fear of death.

The fear of death runs very, very deep and brings countless insights into full consciousness.

When you succeed in really reconciling yourself with death, then your life will definitely become more peaceful, free of drama, more relaxed, and satisfying. Of this I can assure you.

DEATH & THE SPIRITUAL WORLD

Does death actually exist in the spiritual world? Or is the "death-life" axis a phenomenon that exists only on Earth as a by-product of our polarity consciousness?

Yes, the phenomenon death, as well as the phenomenon pain, do exist in the spiritual world. Yet, as a rule, they are handled differently. I hesitate to say they are generally handled better. However, it might be interesting for people to hear a few anecdotes regarding how the spiritual world deals with the phenomenon of death.

As on Earth, there are also different frequency levels at work in the spiritual world. We have the astral world, the causal world, and also the world in which oneness is living reality. I would like to describe this world as the spiritual level. It is also important to note here that there are not better or worse levels. Rather, there are areas in which souls can collect various experiences. Experiencing oneself in different environments is a great joy for the soul. It is an even greater joy to master the different levels. By master, I mean familiarizing oneself (and working with) the laws on each level, as well as creatively expressing oneself within them. That is each soul's highest goal: Creative self-expression. For it is this quality that most especially corresponds to God.

On the astral level, dying is very similar to that on Earth. As on Earth, dying is a very emotional matter, and the fear of "afterward" is very definitive there as well. The astral world is comparable to earth, and is actually the non-material equivalent of earthly existence. Many dramas, injuries, and disappointments occur on that level too, because the feeling of being separate and being different are very dominant in the astral realm. There, injuries to the ego have almost the same repercussions as they do on Earth—with the distinction that this feeling of being separate happens on the nonmaterial (as opposed to material) level. That is why I can say that the fear of death, dying, and the uncertainty of what happens after death, are very closely related.

On the causal level, things look quite different.

This level is mainly inhabited by beings who have mastered Earth and its numerous challenges, thereby freeing themselves from the chains of both the earthly and astral dramas. While individuality does exist there, it is not a result of separation. Rather, it's based on the premise that each soul has a different (and individual) path, within this world. The causal world is a world with endlessly beautiful colors, moving forms, and the possibility of souls merging for a moment and then continuing again on their individual journeys.

I am currently in the process of getting used to the causal world, and becoming familiar with its laws—similar to the way a newborn on earth incarnates step by step into earthly laws.

Naturally, I am very interested in finding out how death works on this frequency. I have already realized: *FEAR OF DEATH DOES NOT EXIST.* If I were to tell the beings here about being extinguished forever, they would laugh, as this reality simply does not exist. It is unthinkable here. According to my research, that is a major difference between the astral and the causal world: The fear of death, which is of great importance and influence in the astral world, simply does not exist on the causal level. You can imagine that I have a wonderful sense of well-being on this level.

You would be amazed to learn about the many beings who have died and come back over and over again. Of course, they do not come back into the same material body they occupied before. They keep coming back as spiritual beings to assist, support, attempt to present solutions, comfort, accompany, and love. The help from the spiritual world is immense. Whoever knows to accept this help definitely leads a fuller life. The life in the hereafter is very rich, colorful and comprehensively fulfilling.

In descriptions of the spiritual world, the same principle applies as to a journalist covering an event in a foreign country: Subjectivity. Depending on the topic, every journalist's report is both highly individual and different. Subjective awareness is even stronger on the causal level than it is on Earth for the following reasons: On earth, material aspects provide a strict and clear framework. In the causal realm, there is much more flexibility. Individual perception is something very normal. Whoever encounters another being here might see that being in quite another way from the being standing next to me, say in other colors and forms. Something like objective truth does not exist on the causal plane. There is only subjective perception. This is indeed a huge area for practice. Scientists don't have an easy time of it on the causal plane, because empirical proof does not exist. In addition, no one there is interested in empirically based proof. Inner truthfulness or pure intent are the qualities that are worked on in the causal world. To exist out of pure God-intention—to create and delight other beings with that—is a central theme of this realm. Concepts like intrigue (or lies) cannot exist in the causal world. There is no space, no foundation, for lies to thrive. That is why mistrust does not exist here either. There are always variations, thousands of options. But there are no lies. A lie, or living a lie, or just covering up the truth—all these live in the realm of the earthly and astral worlds. In the causal spheres there is not so much as a whisper of such a possibility.

The inhabitants of the causal spheres do have the option to return to the astral realm, to work there, and to teach beings who are developing themselves on that level. Yet for many, it makes little sense to go back to a level where they struggled, suffered, and felt lonely for so long. Sometimes there are inner tasks, such as leading beings back to the astral or earthly world. Or maybe there is a deep soul connection with beings who are still embodied, or are at home in a nonmaterial body on the astral level. It is very important that the various levels are not seen in a hierarchical manner, but rather as developmental fields. In the causal world, better and worse do not exist. There, existence reigns with its infinite forms of creative expression. Beings who exist (and feel totally at home) in the astral realm are frequently extremely bored on the causal level—which illustrates the point that so much harmony and consensus is not for everyone!

DO WE RESONATE WITH DEATH?

Even death wants to be mastered. It is important here to distinguish between mastery and inattention, while at once not confusing mastery with ignoring death.

Ignorance is an excellent tool when, for example, a destructive mechanism needs removal. This mechanism can be weakened and extinguished through non-attention. On the other hand, overall ignorance—characterized by fear of confrontation and conflict—does nothing to resolve the challenge of death. Death wants to be met head on and mastered rather than vanquished so that the end result is togetherness rather than opposition.

Truly integrating death into life is very often a remarkable final exam for souls that are developing themselves on Earth. Because death is such an unimaginably frightening concept surrounded by countless myths and strange images, it is not easy for humans to engage with death most of the time. This is so because time and again, the fear germinates that engaging with death will extinguish us. Thus, many people decide, often unconsciously, to stay clear of this subject. However, we humans are now faced with the task of becoming intimate with death, looking death in the eyes, and integrating it into the rich fabric of our soul aspects. What am I trying to say here?

If death is really accepted, even loved, it becomes a servant to people. And people can then bring death into situations where it can be used for transformative processes.

Because human beings and death are so far apart from each other, getting closer is a great challenge, and one that must be faced consciously. In the following, you will find a mantra to work with that supports you in bringing deeply hidden soul contents into consciousness.

I would like to ask you to bring your attention deep inside yourself and simply allow the following questions, observations, and pointers to resonate within you. Let some time pass between each comment. Take the time to listen to your breath. Try to feel within your body what comes up in response to the following words:

Part I

- I hate death.
- Death is the greatest enemy that exists in my life.
- Death repeatedly takes everything from me—especially that which I love.
- Death and I are in endless competition with each other.
- I am always the loser as far as death is concerned.

- I would prefer that death did not exist.
- Death is more powerful than I am.
- Death brings me to my knees.
- Death is cruel.
- Death separates and is merciless.
- Death is my last exit gate.

Part II

- Death comforts me.
- The presence of death helps me to bear this terrible existence on Earth.
- Death protects me because all things are mortal.
- I will be happy when everything is over and death comes knocking on my door.
- Death is a lifesaver.

These sentences do not need to be logically analyzed in your head. Instead, they work from the level of soul, and describe energy qualities that are embedded there. You only need to discover which sentences resonate at that level within your being. Through this exercise, a lot of work will have already occurred.

THE RED THREAD IN LIFE

There are countless ways of going through life. There are thousands of ways, and each person can only discover for himself what he needs to do (or not do) to come into true harmony with his soul's purposes.

If someone experiences deep satisfaction on his life path from the depths of his being again and again, then it follows he cannot then be on a so-called false path.

In the end, the false path doesn't exist because every being carries from within both the tendency and the incontrovertible matrix to distance oneself from God in order to approach him anew. Earthly existence can be reduced to this very simple maxim. At the same time, it also allows for endless variation. Even when the bottom-line is the same for all beings, the path is completely idiosyncratic.

Basically, an earthly incarnation is about contacting one's own red thread of inner determination. Often it takes years, if not decades, to contact this red thread. If a true connection to one's own red thread is present, it does not necessarily mean that one's continued existence is dominated by a string of happy occurrences. When a person has come into contact with his red thread—his SOUL WISH—he then knows what he has to do. This does not mean that what he has to do, and (very importantly) not do, is easy.

If someone sees himself confronted by obstacles in his path, his usual tendency is avoidance. He may attempt to go backward, or avoid the confrontation by taking another path. This is very human because humans like being comfortable. Each time he is confronted by an obstacle, he is also challenged to conjure all his creativity, power, and courage to work through the obstacle, see through it, and finally leave it behind.

If this dynamic—prolonging confrontations with obstacles—has already worked its way into the person's developmental structure, and this person has not yet been able to establish contact with his inner red thread, then the probability is very likely that he will be stuck dealing with one or more obstacles for years. If, however, one has made contact with his inner red thread, then it doesn't mean he will have fewer obstacles on his path. It means that the tendency to avoid and bargain will be discovered much sooner. It could take the form of an uncomfortable feeling overtaking the person that unmistakably reveals the oversight very quickly. Or it could manifest as his life force being reduced, thus forcing him to deal with the hurdle immediately.

The red thread in someone's life is comparable to the needle in a compass pointing the direction. This contact alone with the inner red thread does not constitute walking the path. Yet it does give the person in question a fine feeling for that which is important and unimportant. Through this inner compass, the human increasingly individuates himself from the (outer) currents of the masses, thus approaching the question "What do I actually want? What do I actually need?" These questions are far removed from those deemed important, right, and meaningful by the majority.

Many people are probably capable of knowing, or sensing, the red thread in their lives—perceiving it from a distance. Nonetheless, they fail to both grasp and put it into action—to anchor it in the three-dimensional world. Dissatisfaction always arises out of this discrepancy because the life program does not permit the distance to the red thread to be rewarded through wellbeing and satisfaction. Deep discomfort, displeasure, and dissatisfaction are expressions of not living in inner harmony with the soul's red thread.

In any case, responsibility comes into play at this point. If I have been chronically dissatisfied and sullen for some time (or a lifetime), I can regard this as an inner wake up call to more energetically uncover the red thread, bring it into awareness, and incorporate it into my every day life. An example:

For quite some time, Hanna had a deep desire to have a child with her husband. Fundamentally, she felt very satisfied in her relationship, but the fact that the child for whom she so deeply yearned simply did not want to come, made her very sad. She had actually planned her entire life around becoming a mother and homemaker. She described this wish as the greatest desire of her life. Although she had been very successful in her career, received a respectable salary, and related very well to her colleagues, she still felt something was missing. She assumed she would find satisfaction as a mother—a role for which she had long yearned.

Two years later, there was still no sign she was pregnant. Even though she and her husband frequently consulted a doctor to determine why they were unable to produce a child, the situation remained unchanged.

This situation triggered a life crisis. She no longer knew what meaning her existence could possibly have. She realized that her own mother's life purpose was found mainly through raising her and her three siblings. So when she left home many years later, leaving her mother alone with her father, her mother fell into a crisis and wished deeply to become a grandmother as soon as possible.

Hanna's desire for a child became conflicted: Maybe she didn't even want to have a child? Was she subconsciously trying to derive her inner satisfaction similar to her mother—by having children? Could the answer to these nagging feelings of unhappiness and unfulfilled dreams be found somewhere completely different?

For the first time in her life, Hanna began to ask herself questions that went deeper than those of her parents. She guessed she had to ask herself these questions (and also answer them) with unswerving honesty if she did not want to be surrounded by dark clouds for the rest of her life.

Hanna now began to search for her red thread. She now knew she needed to find the way to herself, her mission, her calling. And thus began a new chapter in her life.

THE RED THREAD & DEATH

From the human point of view, it is understandably difficult to joyfully look forward to something that presents great uncertainty: Death and all that follows.

Even with all the scientific apparatus now available, this question still cannot be answered. There is no physical telephone line between now and the hereafter. There are also no photos from the hereafter. There are, however, many reports from people who have had near-death experiences. There is considerable documentation regarding personal experiences involved in transitioning to the spiritual world. Ironically, this is the crux of the matter: To get closer to death, the threshold of death, and the life that follows death, one cannot use scientific instruments. It is simply not possible to discover these secrets with the aid of computers, analytical thinking, and the examination of (and confrontation with) the physical realm. The only useful means of approaching death and its aftermath, is experience—personal, individual, and subjective experience. Everything else is unworkable.

Death (and the hereafter) will continue to be regarded as frightening images to the world so long as humanity refuses to accept this basic condition.

There are two important factors that must be included in this observation:

1. Dying and death present a transition from the material to the immaterial world.

As banal as this may sound, this is the most important reason why people who concern themselves closely with this subject fail. They try to understand death and what lies beyond from a material point of view, and then project these laws onto the immaterial world. But that doesn't work.

2. That which is hidden behind the threshold of death is already present in life on Earth. But, typically, human beings have not yet connected to this level within themselves.

That is the second essential point that can expedite some hope, for it implies that it is possible to come into contact with that which is beyond death's threshold while at once in human existence.

Whoever only concerns himself with the material level of existence (including human feelings) while alive, cannot help but fear death. For from this vantage point, all that which is perceived as reality is eliminated by the act of death. The body decomposes, and most people assume that the deceased no longer exists. That is a hard pill to swallow and digest. Who wants to die in such a pitiless imaginary climate? No one!

The only ones who can die happily are those who have already concerned themselves (while incarnate) with that which does not get touched by death. Or, put another way, there is an immaterial (red) thread that goes through a person's incarnation. Whoever manages to contact it while still alive, can let it lead him through death into the spiritual world. Contact with the red thread allows for an atmosphere of trust to be present—one in which a person can die in a more relaxed, conscious, and free manner.

When someone has moved along this red thread through death's door, he then finds a huge palette of possibilities.

There is only one irrefutable reality—that I can no longer return to my body. The material shell (body) has to be released. The sooner and more consciously I can release the body, the earlier I can wake up in the spiritual world! Waking up in the spirit world means using non-material sensory organs to take in the new environment, and thereby become more aware of oneself.

Many beings who absolutely don't want to let go of their material bodies find themselves in a condition of inner cloudiness for a very long time. In a way, they are between worlds—because they cannot be in the place they want to be (in their body), and they simultaneously resist going where they are called to be. This creates an in-between condition in which there's little room for play, and where the quality of joy is greatly lacking.

MY PERSONAL EXPERIENCES

My transition to this side was therefore simple, because I was looking forward to experiencing at long last for myself what I had been studying and researching so intensely during my lifetime. For this reason, it was a great adventure. I wanted just one thing: To consciously make the change from one plane to the next. This was my most burning desire, and I succeeded in making it happen.

To flow through the death canal with complete consciousness (and unimpeded by fear), is a tremendous adventure. I don't say that to encourage you from an instructional point of view. I say it out of my own personal experience and inner conviction deriving from this experience.

Therefore, under no circumstances be afraid of dying. Instead, do everything you can during your earthly existence to work through (and release) that which stands in the way of dying consciously. This is my core message to you. It is of utmost importance to me to appeal to you with as much clarity as possible.

As I said, because I was waiting to die at the end of my earthly life and felt death imminent, my level of awareness was very high. "What is going to happen now? Will I also experience the things I heard about from so many near-death reports, or will it be a completely different experience for me?" I asked myself inwardly. I can tell you that it was quite different.

The transition is both a feeling and an experience very difficult to put into words. The vocabulary of languages spoken on Earth is very limited, and therefore barely capable of, aptly communicating the conditions of transitioning into the spiritual world. Much of that which is reality in the spiritual world cannot be expressed in earthly language due to this constraint. Words, as containers of content, always develop out of an experience. Thus, where the experience is absent, so are the corresponding words. All the same, I will now try.

Joyfully anticipating death, I opened all my perceptive faculties to the max. I felt similar to one looking forward to a party or an event; and through this elated anticipation, I was highly receptive to everything coming toward me in the minutes prior to dying. Soon I was able to perceive nonmaterial reality in detail—most especially, a beautiful angelic being who surrounded me with unsurpassed warmth and joy. I was flooded with a feeling that can best be described as *A HOMECOMING.* Simultaneously, there was also a deep disappointment that I had not been able to experience this universal feeling of homecoming during my earthly existence. However, this latter emotion was only of minor significance. It was essential that I could now feel everything with an immensely expanded perception—indescribably open and expansive. It was as if I were finally standing on top of the mountain I had imagined (but was unable to feel) while alive on Earth. Now I was there, standing right in the middle, with an unspeakably beautiful panorama unfolding before me.

Even more than the view of the nonmaterial world, I was deeply touched by the view into my own soul while at once in the midst of it. The beauty of my soul—that I had never been able to sense in such splendor while incarnated on Earth—was suddenly now completely revealed. It was as if I could suddenly be the entire house that I am, and not just the one room I inhabited during my incarnation.

Having come home to my own soul, new events at once followed. Many beings on the other side were anticipating my awakening into the spiritual world with just as much expectation as I experienced on the other side of the "divide." Then suddenly the separation disappeared. And even the idea of separation was totally illusory. In its stead: A hearty welcome. A heartfelt remembrance. An absolute moment of sheer joy.

ASSIGNMENTS CONTINUE

I barely greeted all these beings who were expecting me, when things continued. The spiritual world already had an assignment ready and waiting for me, for which I was initiated by a very tall and mighty being. One of my tasks was to accompany and support beings through their awakening who, like me, had recently awoken from earthly reality. These beings in my charge were still very fear-based, thus causing their awakening process to be considerably prolonged.

Even though I was surprised by how quickly new tasks were being given to me, this task was another delight among all the beautiful experiences in my new environment. Honestly speaking, I wouldn't have minded continuing to simply celebrate with my loved ones in soulful connection. But my guidance had other ideas.

What do you gain if I offer my experiences from the other side, using Bruno as a channel? Is it not so that these images I'm offering might perhaps prevent you from having your very own death experience?

My motivation in sharing these experiences with you is simply to remove fear. There is no other reason. Because fear, which is being made clear to me within the work I am doing on the "other side," can indeed ruin everything. The countless gifts that death holds for those who cross over cannot be received when fear is the dominant factor in this passage. What's more, the transformation process is diminished by the domination of fear. Above all: The joy on this happy occasion— which by far exceeds the intensity and joy that comes at the birth of one's own child—cannot be experienced and felt. And that is such a shame.

So, I want to say to you above all else: Be happy about this far-reaching experience called death. Practice dying during your lifetime as often as you can (i.e., let charac-teristics of your own being die). And just let go of the negative images that you associate with death.

The pain of not being physically close to people who are still incarnated is yet another terrifying association with death. For example, in the beginning, while still in this in-between stage—having not yet grasped the entirety of the spiritual world—it was difficult for me not to be able to speak with my son. It was hard not to be able to sim-ply take him in my arms and say, "Look, I am still here.... Please be aware of me in my present form."

Occasionally, I succeeded in touching the hearts of people whom I loved very much. And for a few seconds, I was able to feel an intimacy that was almost not possible in physical form. However, as I mentioned, I initially suf-fered from physical separation. Yet, with each additional awakening into the spiritual world, with each new dis-covery, and with each newly found joy, this pain soon subsided.

MY EXPERIENCES WITH THOSE WHO HAVE RETURNED

In my field of work, we speak of those who have come back. On Earth, one speaks of those who have passed on. You see it always depends on one's vantage point. For example, I work in the 'receiving station' here—just like someone on Earth who works in a hospital, a nursing home, or as a cashier in a supermarket. There are numerous beings at the receiving station. We joke a lot and have a great deal of fun. The most exhausting beings by far are those who don't want to let go of the Earth at any cost, and who are absolutely determined that things will continue just as they did before. On Earth, one would call these beings abnormally reticent to change. Here, they are known as the Earthbound.

Naturally, it is painful to leave dear habits behind. Naturally it takes time to master this transition. But those on Earth who've categorically rejected any idea of life after death, and are not yet ready to revise their fixed ideas, have it the toughest in the spiritual world.

First of all, they're quite astounded they still exist, especially since they were always utterly convinced they would be completely annihilated. Next, they're very disappointed when it is not the way they had imagined it to be. Then the drama begins: I want this, I want that, and everything is in relationship to earthly reality, which is no longer relevant in this form. Such beings require years adjusting to their existence in the spiritual world.

There is also a category that we jokingly call "purgatory lot." Those are the ones that have just opened their eyes in the spiritual world expecting only to be punished.

If this notion is not carried out, then all their concepts are shaken.

I could go on for hours recounting events that take place in my field of work. And I assure you it wouldn't be boring. Yet, I must point out here that this is primarily not about listening to stories from Elisabeth's treasure chest. Instead, it's about getting to the bottom of your ideas about death.

AREAS OF RESPONSIBILITY

In the spiritual world, too, there are assignments, and areas of assignment. And even specialists who are the absolute best in their field. There are also groups of beings who come together for very special activities, such that (for a period of time) their individuality is almost completely surrendered in order to successfully complete a task.

In the spiritual world, there are broader possibilities for collecting experiences than on Earth. It is basically already clear upon arrival what tasks are ready to be assumed. There are exceptions. For example, if someone had a serious illness while on the earthly plane, they may cure it in the spiritual world. It also sometimes happens that when the physical body dies, the task of an illness is completely accomplished, and the nonmaterial body is immediately freed of numerous ailments. The palette on this level is enormous. It would take far too long to describe it all, and I don't want to tell you everything in advance.

Another one of my areas of responsibility is to make sure that people are able to let go of their fear of death. In this regard, I capitalize on using my name: Elisabeth Kübler-Ross. Many people know this name, so I want to take advantage of its familiarity by saying "Unless one wants to continue believing in this old fairy tale, dying and death are not terrible." For this reason I will again closely examine what 'ingredients' are necessary in order to make a successful transition from this side to the other.

The core point on which more than 50% of the success depends is this: Fear. How deep is death still connected to fear in me? Please allow this question to really sink in. As far as I am concerned, how deeply is death still connected to fear?

If death and fear entertain a "symbiotic relationship" within me, then I can assume that I will probably not get to experience the joy that is connected to death when I change planes. Therefore, the most damaging ingredient to the dying and death process is fear. However, if I take a large leap of faith, and allow myself to be accompanied by this quality through the dying process, then the prognosis for a successful transformation is very good. If I add to that trust a large dose of self-love, then nothing more will impede a joyful transition to the other side.

I maintain: A minimum of fear, and a maximum of trust and self-love can elevate dying to the crowning pinnacle of an incarnation. In addition—and this seems rather important to me—if one is also dedicated, then nothing more can go wrong. Self-love, trust and dedication are at once the gentlest and the best qualities that are required for a successful transition. It is up to me to decide how many of these qualities are available to me during my lifetime.

Just as ripe tomatoes, onions, garlic, and a good broth are necessary ingredients for a good spaghetti sauce, I can say with certainty: Dedication, trust and self-love are essential for a successful dying process!

THE SEEMINGLY IMPENETRABLE BORDER

Why is it that on Earth the nonmaterial plane is predominantly not perceived at all? What purpose does the wall serve that separates this side from the hereafter? Is this divine misdirection, or is it merely part of the separation drama that humankind has chosen for itself?

From my point of view, separation serves the same purpose as classroom walls—allowing one to better concentrate on solving the exercises assigned by the teacher. Because people do not also have to concern themselves with the vastness of the nonmaterial world, greater focus on the material to be learned can take place. On the one hand, there are numerous beings who suffer a great deal under these fixed borders that separate the worlds. They are mainly beings who have recently suffered many painful experiences, who delved deeply into the darker side of earthly life, and who carry heavy trauma within their cells. They yearn to be able to break through these stubborn borders. But contact with the nonmaterial world, as an escape from Earth's harsh realities, is not beneficial for development in general. However, expanding beyond the boundaries between this side and the hereafter is beneficial. The point being that this expansion would first allow people to naturally develop a relationship with this border, and subsequently move beyond it. This makes things much easier.

If we look at the overall development of humanity, we can see progressive movement in the direction of supplanting separation in favor of unification. This is a development that humanity is undertaking in partnership with Mother Earth. Borders are falling, and territorial boundaries that create hostility are being loosened under the motto: "One Earth, one world."

It is a development that requires time. When the thought of oneness, the reality of oneness, gradually moves through the borders between countries, then it is just a matter of time until the knowledge "we are one cosmos" pervades the entire world. In truth, "we are one cosmos" dissolves the boundaries between the nonmaterial and material worlds.

The Earth is gradually developing in a direction beyond a representational "lesson planet" where very difficult life lessons must be learned. Rather, it is becoming a planet that holds many opportunities for learning that have to do with matter.

A very important learning opportunity is the fact that matter is not separate from spirit, and vice versa. When that is both understood and experienced, then the collaboration between the angelic realm and the human realm becomes an everyday reality.

Yet until then there is quite a lot to do. Until then, there are many boundaries one must learn to love and, by so doing, make both permeable and penetrable.

DEATH IN THE SPIRITUAL WORLD

As previously mentioned, death does exist in the spiritual world—though not in the sense that a physical body dies and one believes in the illusion that he *is* the physical body. No, death has completely different qualities in the spiritual world. And you know me, I won't let up until I have really understood death on the spiritual plane as well. My research has definitely brought me much farther. But I must tell you that there is still much that puzzles me. Let me give you an idea of some of these questions:

- What purpose does death have in the spiritual world when the spiritual world is so much closer to life?

- Why can someone also die in the spiritual world where dying is seen as an illusion?

- Is dying a means of getting closer and closer to life (God) in the spiritual world too

Those are just a few of the questions I have. And hopefully with time there won't be as many.

DYING & DEATH IN THE SPIRITUAL WORLD

When one speaks of death on Earth, generally the death of the body is what is meant. In our deliberations, we have discovered that death does not only work in the dying of the physical body, but is also involved in the minute details of everyday human life.

In the spiritual world, death doesn't exist as such because the consciousness is present that life always continues. The assumption that there could be no more existence after death has no foundation in the spiritual world—at least not in the areas in which I move. Here, death exists only in the sense of disintegration and new beginnings. That is a natural law that creates many blessings and considerable joy. It is present on my level of development for this reason. Moments die, situations die. But—and this is the most important difference—the awareness that life is eternal never dies!

A person does not live on Earth automatically, without his participation in the reality of eternity. If someone wants to integrate the consciousness of eternity into his everyday life, a great deal of work is necessary. In the spiritual world this is not necessary. The notion of eternity is very normal and natural here, so it is questionable whether a person is all right who claims that life is limited. Those beings who question the concept of eternal life in the spiritual world are holding onto an outside position. To be more exact: In the same way that limitation is the norm in earthly reality, eternity is the norm in the spiritual world. You can imagine that the consciously felt (and uninterrupted presence of) eternity can produce a unique generosity.

For example, if something does not go as planned and a delay occurs, then the notion of death does not appear as the uncompromising executor of imminent demise, demanding homage. Instead, eternity spreads its arms and says, "You still have an eternally long time to actualize this."

As you can imagine, it is not always easy to deal with eternity, for it is without end. For me personally, it was a huge switch from earth-time reality to that of spiritual-eternal truth.

PREVENTING DEATH

Delaying death is the primary preoccupation of many people. Ultimately, many activities are based on this principle. I do not doubt this principle. It is also good that it has an effect on Earth. Without this principle, people would forget to eat, to take care of their bodies, and much more.

In the spiritual world, where the motivational force "delaying death" is barely present, another type of motivational force is needed. This too was a big change for me, as I was occasionally irritated because I had no motivation to move forward. I couldn't be bothered to do this or that anymore because I was in an indescribably blissful state. On reflection, I discovered it wasn't merely this all-encompassing joy that affected my motivation. It was also the fact that I did not have to run away from anything. It then became clear to me that the flight from death—the flight from being extinguished—caused a tremendous flurry of activity. What's more, that same activity (not motivated by love) was actually useless—except maybe to prevent, delay, or bar death.

Perhaps you might occasionally catch yourself building a memorial in the world. It may be through a great invention, a literary bestseller, or simply through a life-size sculpture of yourself. Whenever that happens, the fear of death is always present. Whenever I erect monuments to myself, I fight against the fact of impermanence, without knowing that impermanence is a superficial condition. My true being is immortal.

TRANSITIONING FROM THE MATERIAL TO NONMATERIAL EXISTENCE

Each time I describe the transition, I am actually referring to parts of it. The transition is so all encompassing and exuberant, I can only address various aspects of this pervasive experience, filter them through my consciousness, and then relate them to you.

Actually, dying was not a transition. It was more of an expansion and the release of a limitation. My true being did not really change through the experience of death. Death only affects the outer personality. And I can assure you that characteristics previously limiting on the earthly plane suddenly had no more significance. It was an experience of renewal and purification.

However, the fear was still there that by casting off the old worldly habits I would become completely separated from my beloved family. I was afraid I would lose my place as a family member if I were to let go of personality traits (like my stubbornness) that had previously given me support. As this process of releasing my worldly identity was near completion, something happened that I would like to call a *MIRACLE*.

By letting go of my worldly personality traits, I entered into a condition of all-encompassing *LOVE*. I had the feeling of being closer than ever to my children and my sister. And that was very, very beautiful.

ENTERING NEW TERRITORY

Awakening in the spiritual world step by step is very special. On the one hand, because my human perception was still somewhat present, it was completely new and unknown to me. On the other hand, it was a long-lasting kind of déjà-vu—one in the midst of the unknown. This experience caused turmoil within me. This condition reminded me of my youth, when so many new things overwhelmed me while simultaneously past experiences and preconceived ideas resisted giving way.

But, and I want to emphasize this again here: Awakening in the spiritual world is wonderful. As I awoke in this beautiful bright environment, I was totally overwhelmed by the diversity of impressions that flooded me. I asked myself what was really different in the spiritual world, and came to this conclusion: The total absence of fear. That is the biggest difference. Just imagine: No fear exists in my present sphere! That is the biggest gift that existence in the spiritual world offers.

Whether you believe it or not: In the beginning I actually missed fear a little. Although at the time of my existence on Earth I wasn't an especially fearful person, I did perceive the difference between the fearful atmosphere on Earth, and the fearless environment in the spiritual world very intensely.

From my current perspective, it is almost impossible to experience this complete fearlessness on Earth. In the atmosphere of everyday life on Earth a certain form of basic fear is always present. To avoid being affected by this fear during one's lifetime seems almost impossible to achieve.

Please do not mistake my observation as a criticism of your doing something wrong. No, it is just the reality of different environments. When changing from one level to another, these differences are experienced especially powerfully and vividly.

To be honest, I have to admit that it is not much fun for me to travel to Earth for the aforementioned reason. Although it moves me and gives me feelings of belonging to visit my loved ones, the constriction of fear in Earth's vibrational field, often takes the joy out of the journey there for me.

Bruno has asked if I would be available for others to speak to me when the book is published. Because I really want to settle into my present home and anchor myself here, I have decided this is not an opportune time.

Going back and forth between these worlds requires tremendous strength and is not that easy. It is comparable to the challenge a human faces when going back and forth between South Africa and Siberia on a daily basis, constantly having to adjust to climatic, time zone, and cultural conditions.

The nicest, of course, is when I travel to earth and am perceived there. It is a truly wonderful experience for me when I visit my dear ones and they perceive my presence and speak to me. While this is not essential, it is still important to me to be treated like a living being and not like an *old memory*. Being perceived and accepted as real, rather than viewed as deceased and forever extinguished, makes it easier for me to touch their hearts.

I can assure you that someone from the spiritual world is always with you, provided you are not totally closed off and thereby unavailable for nonmaterial energies. Imagine that—always! When you feel alone, the only reason for this is because your heart is closed. The heart is the place of contact where the material and the nonmaterial worlds most completely and directly meet and merge.

Bruno has just gone through a period of doubt. For about two days he asked me to prove that I am really Elisabeth. It would be easy to deliver any old proof that I am really she. But to obtain proof when you are in contact with someone from the spiritual world is not the point. The important thing is the feeling in your heart, and the quality of what occurs when you open yourself to this world. The law of resonance works in the spiritual world just as it does in earthly reality. The contact between Bruno and me came about because he wanted to write a book, and I simultaneously had a few things to share. In addition we are also able to meet on a suitable vibrational frequency.

The exceptional part is that my last incarnation was not that long ago. That makes our collaboration on the one hand easier, because parts of my consciousness are still closely connected with the Earth. On the other hand, it is challenging to keep returning to the place to which I am actually saying goodbye.

Therefore, do not consider dying and death as a strong tug-of-war where, from one moment to the next, everything is completely different. Instead, imagine a flowing transition. It takes some time before the being completely arrives at the new level with all of its many different parts. This is somewhat similar to returning home from a vacation with strong impressions and experiences, feeling as if you are still somewhat away. Parts of your being remained there. Calling those parts back step by step into the here-and-now takes time. The same applies to transition from this side to the hereafter.

Although many things are very different in the spiritual world, a lot is also exactly the same. This has to do with the fact that ultimately the two worlds are not separate from one another. Only the illusory wall of separation gives you the feeling that it is otherwise. The earthly and spiritual world basically consist of the same substance—love!

In the same way that during my time on Earth the Berlinwall was torn down, the time is getting closer when the wall between the spiritual and the earthly world will be eliminated. This is because it becomes increasingly permeable, until it no longer makes any sense.

Until now, it was very important to maintain this boundary because the hard lessons of life needed the tightly woven frame of time and space created by the demarcation of death. Otherwise, all humans would have wandered into the world of pure spirit in order to avoid the hurdles that life presents for their further development.

The more you have access to the meaning of these hurdles in your life path, the less interest you will have in avoiding them. The more you are in contact with the life plan deep within you, the less danger there is of neglecting your life lessons due to the expanded playing field of the spiritual world. In this sense, I can say that to the extent a human is able to understand the meaning of his lessons, to that exact extent will he be allowed to penetrate into the spiritual world and come in contact with nonmaterial beings. They are often beings with whom he may have spent a shorter or longer time on Earth, but who are now at home in the nonmaterial world.

It is now insignificant where a being is, after all—in the earthly world, or in the hereafter. What is significant is the effort to come ever closer to the origin of life. To come ever closer to true love. Beings in the spiritual world are just as challenged as you are in this regard. It is about the same theme: Coming closer to the divine within your own being, exploring the miracle of the divine ever more deeply. And most of all, using your own divine creativity for the blessing of all. In the spirit world too there are also lessons and learning experiences waiting for you. That does not change when you switch planes.

My lesson at the moment consists of remaining in contact with myself, even though I move around 'externally' in various environments. Additionally, a side task is that I relive sequences of my earthly life in order to work through and reabsorb them into my expanded consciousness, thereby integrating them.

Since man is "fighting on the front line" in a certain

sense during his earthly existence, a very high density of experience is created. It makes sense to harvest this density of experience and transform it afterward in the vastly expanded consciousness of the spiritual world.

Depending on how high the experience density was in the last incarnation, a soul will have more or less to work through and lift into expanded consciousness. I can tell you that is a very exciting activity. Because many connections, unrecognizable during the incarnation (at least, not recognizable to me) suddenly appear in the spiritual world in a crystal clear light. It now becomes completely clear why things happened the way they did during earthly times. Self-love can always be well measured by how far someone is ready to stand by other beings in their development. I have purposely avoided the word "help" because in the end, each person can only help himself. That however is yet another subject.

My very practical work here takes the form of standing by beings incarnating from the Earth into the spiritual world. It is similar to the process a child goes through during its incarnation on Earth: Manifesting its own being step by step in the new environment. Just as there are birthing clinics on Earth, there are also birthing clinics in the so-called hereafter. In these "clinics" beings are supported in finding their way into, and arriving at, their new environment. It is a very interesting task. Because I was involved with exiting the earthly world while

I was there, the obvious next step is to concern myself with entrance to the hereafter. I am now on "the other side of the tunnel" so to speak, and experience things embedded in the so-called "hereafter."

This work was entrusted to me because I had already overcome the fear of dying while I was living on Earth. Only for that reason was it possible for me, upon awakening in the spiritual world, to be able to support others relatively quickly as they made their entrance into this level of existence.

Do you have a question about this work Bruno?

B: Is this work fun for you, and how much do you earn?

E: You are great fun today.

B: Yes, well, let me shorten the question to: Is it fun for you to work like this?

E: Yes, this is a lot of fun for me. Through the disappearance of the material level, *that which is* appears much clearer. I can more quickly grasp what is going on with a newcomer. The reality in which he finds himself is more or less delivered to me on a silver platter. This has to do with the fact that the spirit is no longer hidden by matter. The truth cannot be covered up on my level of existence. Therefore, no lie can be present. There is nothing that can cover up the truth—*that which is*. There is no secret place where something can be hidden, and which no one is allowed to see. There are no secrets. Because of that, it also never happens that something comes to light slowly. There is only *that which is*. I still have to get used to that. On Earth I had (and wanted) to hold certain things back now and again—either because I didn't trust the other person to handle what I was holding back, or simply because I wanted to keep things to myself.

Here, where I am now at home, other beings are able to understand me as well as I understand myself. In many encounters, this led to special situations. I was still very much influenced by my earthly existence, and tried to restrain excitement in my new environment. It was just silly because the other being was immediately able to perceive what I was trying to hold back, and addressed it with me. On the earthly plane this would have been experienced as highly embarrassing. In the spiritual world, it is just the way it is.

For this reason, there are far fewer intricacies. There is no need to deceive, to manipulate, and to lie. Rather, it is about bearing witness to that which is, and to enjoy it. The energy that is not wasted on games of hide-and-seek (and other time-consuming deceptions) can therefore flow into joy. The joy of original existence. A joy that, like a birthright, is simply there. A joy similar to a sound that never fades away.

That does not preclude challenges from presenting themselves, or even being subjected to excessive demands. But this sound is present at the same time—the eternal sound of joy. I am often amazed that this sound of joy is constantly present. When I was able to perceive this joy, those were my greatest moments on Earth. It lasted for two or maybe three days, and would then be overshadowed by an unpleasant event. Here, this original joy cannot be covered up. It is simply here, and accompanies me into my learning experiences. And because this joy is constantly present in the depths of my being, many challenges are mastered with a wonderfully great portion of humor. To immerse oneself for days on end in any problem is not possible, for the sound of joy breaks up this game very quickly. *I am in joy* is a daily living reality here.

MERGING INTO ONE BEING

Through shedding the human body, it becomes easier to experience oneself as a divine being. The monumental guilt complex that burdens the shoulders of all humanity melts, and the divine is as normal and real as the air you breathe on Earth. As I said before, in no case should you assume that a paradise-like land of milk and honey is waiting for you where there is nothing left to do. Here too there is much that can be shifted and changed, motivated not so much from the viewpoint that things are not good as they are, but rather in order to be close to love by serving love. This is a fundamentally different motivation.

Mostly, we are aware that we cannot really change *that which is*. We can, however, bring the love that lives within us to full expression with the possibilities that are available to us. In this regard, individual beings have different possibilities. If, however, just one being suppresses his individual possibility for expressing love, then something is missing.

Right now, I am not the only one who is speaking to Bruno. Four other beings are also present with me. I can tell you that it is very uplifting to release one's own individuality in order to create one being that consists of five individual beings. Then, when this dance-of-five has danced to an end, we will dissolve this bond and let ourselves be led by the wave of love into the next adventure.

You too may be familiar with this experience when you enter a creative process in the company of people you like very much. It can then happen that your nonmaterial bodies join together and, out of this union, something totally new is created. Something that no one could have created by himself, something unique, made possible through the presence of these particular participants.

There are beings (and by this I also mean people) who are almost addicted to being carried by an uplifting group vibration. Yet, an uplifting, joyful group atmosphere on Earth can only be created when people are sufficiently deeply in touch with themselves. But if someone has lost touch with himself and tries to find comfort in the group instead, then the group experience is very much reduced. If, however, that person is in harmony with his own being, and in touch with himself, then he can experience ecstatic moments within the group.

I would love to invite you to participate in the dance that we are dancing at this moment. It is a dance of joy. This concludes the section of Elisabeth with her spirit brothers and sisters.

WHEN ENERGIES MERGE

Have you also had the experience of stewing for hours over a problem? You search desperately for the solution. You want to solve this problem at any cost because a lot depends on it. Yet the solution does not reveal itself, try as you might. So you put the problem aside and go and talk to your dear friend about something else entirely. All of a sudden, a lightbulb goes off, and the solution is there. Why is the solution suddenly there?

Through your conversation you created a new atmosphere. This new, more relaxed field, coupled with the exact quality your friend contributed during that moment in the conversation (without knowing it), was necessary for the solution to arise and the lightbulb moment to happen. The solution was not able to surface in an atmosphere dominated by will ("I want to find the answer right now!").

The same principle applies when you come into contact with non-incarnated beings. In the best case scenario, they are able to send out the exact same energy form you need in order to close the circle, to find the missing puzzle piece, or to flip the switch so the light comes on.

It is my deep wish for you to open your heart to the help available from the nonmaterial world. It is not about making the nonmaterial world responsible for the solutions to your problems—that is ultimately always the responsibility of each individual. However, by consciously opening your awareness to help from the spiritual world, many more gateways are created through which solutions can come to you.

INTERVIEW BY ELISABETH

E: Dear Bruno. A lot in this book has been about my world. Much that we have talked about is connected to the universe in which I am now at home. I would like to turn the tables on you and ask, "In what universe do you find yourself at the moment?"

B: How nice that someone is finally interested in me.... (wink)

E: I gather that life as a medium and therapist includes many sacrifices.

B: Yes, during the sessions, it is never about my problems— as I jokingly referred to before. My clients are seeking solutions to their own problems (which is their right), rather than hearing about mine.

E: Good. So now you will get the chance of a lifetime to air your problems with Elisabeth.

B: Given such a large audience, I feel rather reserved. But since you've asked me so directly, I don't want to miss this opportunity. Do you have a particular question for me?

E: No, I am pleased for you to just talk about yourself, your world and what concerns you at this time.

B: The universe in which I currently find myself is very small on the one hand, but vast on the other. From the vantage point of space, I am moving around in approximately the same small area. From an inner perspective, I am in touch with so many aspects of nonmaterial reality, it brings me right to the edge of being overwhelmed.

Although contact with the spiritual world is strenuous, owing to it always requiring rebalance with the material world, I am now used to it.

A very pertinent issue for me right now is publishing this book.

E: What concerns you then, relating to this?

B: The work with you is special to me insofar as you've recently lived in a body on Earth and have therefore left a trail behind. As such, contact with you is more immediate, and thus more powerfully reduces the boundary between the here-and-now and the hereafter.

I have already been in contact with beings on the other side for many years. However, in my work with you, we are co-creating a tangible product for the rest of my fellow man.

My intention and my desire is that the crossing of the border between here-and-now and the hereafter will finally be freed from the magical nonsense that surrounds it, and become something very natural.

It is both my intention and desire to finally see the veil between the here-and-now and the hereafter freed from the illusionary nonsense surrounding it, in order to evolve into something very natural.

E: Yes, that is what this is all about. Each time someone breaks through the barrier between this world and the hereafter (while not being held back by the common belief "they are crazy. Now they are extremely delusional"), then they are able to work very profoundly on the subject of death. And, as you have said, an essential effect lies in this contact between the worlds becoming the most natural thing there is!

B: However, I ask myself if I will ever experience that.

E: Look, you are working on helping this reality of non-separation to manifest more and more. I can let you in on the fact that, on the spiritual level, *SCORES* of beings are making a huge effort to lift this border. Yet—and this is an essential point—the efforts on our side are less relevant than those on yours. It is no problem for us to connect to earthly reality. It is questionable though whether this is interesting and joyful for us. For many beings in the hereafter, after a certain point of feeling our existence is being ignored, it is not particularly edifying to travel the path into those dense structures, including approaching the fear structures surrounding Earth.

Often, small openings in people suffice that can considerably raise the fun quotient for nonmaterial beings. But more often it is like talking to a wall. And that can also be painful!

B: I also experienced a phase when I didn't want to have anymore to do with non-incarnated beings. For one thing, because practical earthly challenges already require all my strength. And for another, because I had my fill of messages that painted such an enticing picture.

E: Do you know of any relationships that don't have anything to do with disappointments, high expectations, frustrations, and maybe even a feeling of no exit? This is also the case with relationships that span the two worlds.

These are not just good-time relationships. These are relationships that require a great deal from both sides. Because we are not incarnated on the physical level (and are not thus burdened by so many constraints), we frequently take on a supportive and protective role toward people. This is possible because we have greater capacities, and because the veil of illusion does not get in our way as much as it does yours.

B: For me, the heart plays an important role between connecting the spiritual and material worlds. In connecting with you, too, I have the feeling that the heart is the main meeting place for our encounters.

E: You said that very beautifully.

B: Yes, it can be said so simply because that is how it is, and also because it answers your question regarding my universe. In all the years I have been working as a medium, the gradual transfer of energy to the heart has been at the core.

The beginning of my work as a medium mainly concerned the channel above my head that reached into the spiritual world. The energies that streamed into me through this channel were expressed as words that came straight from my mouth. Since then, the flow of energy has changed to the degree that it first takes the path to my heart before leaving my mouth as words.

E: The heart is always the central meeting place. It is the central meeting place among people, it is the central meeting place within people, and it is the central meeting place between people and nonmaterial beings.

Why don't you write a book about it?

B: Here we are—back on the subject of so many tasks to be mastered on Earth, with limited time available in which to do them.

E: The important issue is always whether one's main purpose can be found. I consider this as being essential on *EARTH*. Whoever does not find his calling, will not succeed in being truly and deeply happy.

The interesting (and often uncomfortable) thing for many is: No one—but no one—can assume the search and discovery of anyone else's main purpose. Only the person in question is in a position to find and contact his or her calling.

Generally speaking, God is the core. But, how God wants to be expressed through you and your main purpose is another question that only you can answer by digging into the depths of your being. This main purpose is not made completely obvious to anyone. It takes effort. It takes the desire to come into contact with one's purpose.

It takes *COURAGE* to stand by this main purpose and really live it, apart from whatever ideas society may have. How many people do not live their purpose because they fear their fellow man will no longer love them? Please observe that being loved and being tolerated are two different things. I can only be truly loved when I am in contact with my true purpose, while also bringing it into expression. For only those who are in contact with their main purpose are able to love themselves completely.

The main purpose *IS LOVE*.

Do you have any more questions, Bruno?

B: Wow, that is a powerful statement!

E: Do you know where it originates?

B: Yes, from us!

E: Exactly, it doesn't just come from me. It doesn't just come from you. Instead, it arises where the two of us come together and meet.

B: That moves me deeply. And it challenges the boundary between you and me.

E: Yes, parallel to gradually dissolving fear of death, work is done on the wall between people. The separation between the nonmaterial world and the material world is directly connected to the separation between individual people. And I can tell you with conviction that people suffer from the existence of walls that separate them. To a great extent, these separating walls are comprised of fear. From my current perspective, this is very clearly visible. During my earthly incarnation that was not so obvious to me.

B: Now, that brings up sadness in me.

E: Well, it is good that it saddens you. For realities change only when they are felt.

B: I totally agree with you—an essential and fundamental principle in therapeutic work.

E: I can also tell you that purely therapeutic work doesn't do any good if it isn't connected to a spiritual dimension.

B: That is a very drastic statement!

E: Yes, from the perspective that I feel and observe life, this is an essential truth. For illness always arises where there is a distance from God. If I want to heal this illness and not just postpone it, then I must reduce the distance to God; or, respectively, remove it. Here, I am referring to the soul level. As the body always *IS* a reaction to the soul, healing always begins by overcoming the distance to God.

B: In my experience, there seems to be no given way to overcome the distance to God.

E: Yes, I perceive that the same way. Just as the path to one's own purpose is an individual path, the way to reducing the distance to God is also idiosyncratic. Each person has individually distanced himself from God, and each person finds his own individual way back to God.

E: And, dear Bruno, how is it for you? Would you like to end your cycle of incarnation?

B: You are really asking very directly.

E: Why should we avoid this hot topic any longer? It is important to me to address things directly and name them.

B: *Yes, I have the feeling that this is probably my last* incarnation, and I will be happy if I can experience myself as a giving person in this incarnation.

E: That sounds very romantic. But, I want to say to you that, through your death and last earthly incarnation, your experience on Earth is not at an end. The Earth is our main foundation. Those beings who decided to join the Earth cycle a long time ago, who also sank into the deepest darkness during many incarnations on Earth, and then developed themselves and grew beyond Earth, are very deeply connected to the Earth for development. Once the cycle of incarnation is completed, the love for Earth becomes very deep and great. In addition, a deep need arises from within to support the Earth and its inhabitants on their journey into the light.

Especially when there are radical changes in progress, as there now are, the presence of Masters is exceedingly important. By Masters, I mean beings who have gone through the Earth cycle and have lived through all the highs and lows of earthly existence, omitting nothing there is to experience. Through this self-obtained experiential knowledge, the Masters are able to offer effective support, even though they are not authorized to solve the problems of the world. To do so would eliminate the growth potential of the Earth's inhabitants. And that would not serve the development of love.

B: What does your help then look like?

E: First, my help lies in perceiving all these connections from my expanded perspective. At the moment, my practical support is of small consequence as I am still getting used to my new environment. Because forgetting on planet Earth is enormous and deep, I need a lot of strength to reintegrate the forgotten aspects of my own soul. Does that make sense?

B: Yes, I see what you mean.

E: Precisely because I am in the process of anchoring myself even more deeply in the spiritual world, my work with you is limited as far as time or energy goes. My newer incarnation in the spiritual world currently has first priority, which is why I cannot use too much energy contacting the Earth plane.

My task also involves getting even closer to the phenomenon of death and dying. And in the spiritual world, realizations are coming to me faster than ever before. Unlike Earth, realizations don't have to be worked at so hard here. I am very happy to let several people take part in these realizations now. And what is your task, dear Bruno?

B: My assignment involves accompanying people to the depths of their own soul through my therapeutic work as a medium—to a depth that I first worked very hard to achieve myself. Furthermore, my work lies in totally reconciling myself with the world, its laws of nature, and the demanding lessons there are to be learned in the world. That is a central matter of concern to me.

Also, another of my assignments is to disregard and disbelieve in the boundary between the here-and-now and the hereafter, and thereby dismantle it.

E: Doesn't the last assignment you mentioned bring up fear in you?

B: Sure, occasionally it does, but then a moment later I am happy that this fear is revealing itself. Because of that, I am consciously able to release it.

E: I remember these difficult tests very well. My last big test was that death did not occur when I began to yearn for it so much at the end of my life. I therefore experienced the pain that arises when death is not active. That was a very important experience for me, and allowed me to become a Master with regard to death—death that is so dearly wished for but does not show up. This was why I began to really appreciate death. It was neither a mental idea nor a thought construct. Rather, it was a feeling that went through my entire being: "I appreciate you death; and I am pleased when the time comes for you take over my earthly body." That was the final attitude in my earthly existence.

B: Does that still make you sad?

E: Yes, when I talk about it, it still gets under my "nonmaterial" skin.

B: That means it doesn't matter what plane or sphere you are in to be able to experience sadness in the spiritual world, too?

E: Yes, of course. Imagine if it were not possible to mourn events. That would be terrible. Sorrow, as well as death, are instrumental parts of life when used in their appropriate places.

The ability to mourn is a considerable part of being able to let go. Therefore, sorrow and letting go are death's main assistants.

Mourning is an instrument that has to be used at the right time. And it also has to be released at the right time. Too much mourning, or sorrow, can be misused as a device for hiding from life. Properly employed, it can be death's right hand.

B: That sounds a little sterile to me...to employ sorrow.

E: That was meant figuratively. It so happens that the more awareness is present, the more these aspects of existence can be specifically used. Of course, they arise from certain situations. But at the same time, they can be guided:

"Sorrow, you may now arise within me. You are helping me work through this terrible experience. Thank you very much for supporting me." That is how it can sound, for example. This also applies to us in the spiritual world.

B: I am pleased when the boundaries between these worlds continue to get smaller.

E: In the beginning, the removal of these borders will be realized in individuals, and consequently expand to the collective reality. There are no borders between the spiritual and earthly world, unless humans believe in them.

B: Yes, I was just talking with my colleague about the likelihood that, in the future societies' view, it is not those who are in contact with the spiritual world who have a problem, but rather those who do not communicate with the spiritual world who have a problem.

E: Yes, but do be aware that for many people the border between this world and the other is almost necessary for survival. They need this border to be able to find their way in the world! That is why some people become very emotional when this ridged boundary is shaken.

Also, when collective consciousness takes steps toward removing this boundary, know that it can be important for some individuals to maintain it. For this reason the process should happen organically. However, it is also important that those who do go beyond this boundary do not feel ashamed. That is why we are writing this book.

FRUITS OF REALIZATION

B: I find the content you are imparting in regard to death to be very essential. I assume this also has to do with the fact that you were so intensely concerned with this subject matter during your last incarnation?

E: Yes, during my lifetime I worked very intensely with this subject matter. I wrestled with it, fought against it, threw it out, and took it up again. It was really a very far-reaching process. In a certain sense, my soul is still recovering from this intense confrontation. On my present level of existence, I do not have to dig deeply in order to gain that level of insight. Here, insights are like ripe fruit on trees that can easily be picked. These insights are of great significance to me because, deep within the structure of my soul, I know how hard I had to work for this knowledge. That is why they have an enormous value attached to them.

Whereas before I operated so carelessly with these realizations, I have only now become completely aware of their value. It is worth getting to know the adversities on Earth. These adversities are preparing one in a special way for the *Nectar of Spirit*. Through that awareness, I have also realized what a wonderful paradise we are allowed to live in—be it on Earth or the entire universe.

Adam and Eve were not chased out of paradise. No. They forgot that, due to the fateful things they themselves created, they were actually already in paradise. People are in a similar situation. They inhabit paradise. But in the course of millennia, have created such a huge amount of sorrow, mental confusion, and mistrust, they are no longer aware of the paradise in which they live.

How do you see this, Bruno? Are you also of the same opinion?

B: Given my own experience, I know that insights frequently have to be fought for very hard, and that the state of "Now I've got it" can never be fully reached. Whenever I have an unusually enlightening realization, it is often quicklyfollowedbyintensedownhillchallenges.Itreminds me of the roller coaster ride at the fair—Up and down.

The aphorism you mentioned earlier—about man already being in paradise but not being able to recognize or feel it—I can understand that very, very well.

Many adversities come spontaneously to mind. I am thinking of the numerous illusions I have had, or had the opportunity to let go of over the years, for the sake of a deep feeling of wellbeing and a real homecoming from within.

E: What illusions are you referring to?

B: The illusion of believing that I would receive something long term from outside, even if inwardly not yet developed. The illusion that love comes from without, even if not developed from within. The illusion that pain is no longer necessary for learning.

E: In any case, do not hold onto the idea that pain is an important teacher for you. It is a teacher that over time will no longer be required to serve you. That just takes time. But I can tell you one thing: You do not need pain until the "end of your development." That is also an illusion: The end of development, eh?

It was a great pleasure for me to work with you. You are a terrific vessel, and you have a wonderful body that is easily able to absorb and purely reproduce what it is I want to share. Because of this, we have a lot of envious beings up there, who would also like to have such a great medium. Naturally, I know you do not just want to be a medium. Although, regarding our project, you are that about 75% of the time. And that is good. Otherwise, you would have to work even more. And I certainly don't want to burden you with any more work.

Now, I want to go and visit my beloved relatives for a while. From my heart, I wish you a happy and relaxed evening.

– *Elisabeth*

Glossary

[1] Channel

The spiritual energetic connection to the supernatural world. A connection that goes from the heart through the crown chakra upward. It is perceived as a channel of light.

[2] Elisabeth Kübler-Ross

Born July 8, 1926, Zurich, Switzerland. Died August 24, 2004, Scottsdale, Arizona. She was a Swiss-American psychiatrist. She specialized in death and dying, mourning and bereavement, and is considered the founder of research on death and dying.

[3] Medium (Person)

A person, who transmits messages from supernatural beings, such as angels, spirits, or people who have died before us.

In the 70's, the American New Age Movement coined the term Channeling to refer to this concept. It was later adapted in German in the 80's.

Many followers of religious movements and world religions are convinced that their holy scriptures were transferred from gods or angels to specifically chosen people (mediums) either in part or completely.

[4] Channeling

When, through the channel, information and energies from different levels of consciousness—or being—are expressed or received.

[5] Incarnation

Embodiment.

The process by which a spiritual, nonmaterial being/soul takes on a bodily form.

[6] Mantra

Holy syllables and holy texts that, through repetition, reveal their power and also have a calming, focusing, and strengthening effect on people that supports their development.

In our time, the same concept is also used for affirmations, which equally serves strengthening, healing and unfolding.

[7] Excarnation

The process by which the soul leaves the body for good.

ENETECHIEL– here and now

This second volume of ENETECHIEL is about the work of the angelic being in groups and in individual sessions. The reader is invited to undertake a journey into the innermost realms of self. Authentic group sessions, guided meditations and lessons by ENETECHIEL are the tools of this journey. We can thereby recognize ourselves mirrored in one another.

The enclosed CD is both an adjunct to and continuation of that inner journey. ENETECHIEL provides us with highly efficient tools to connect to our true being, thus allowing us to address concrete daily life questions and practical issues such as decision-making.

»ENETECHIEL – hier und jetzt«
Elraanis-Verlag 2004, Hardcover, 224 S.
with Meditations-CD
ISBN 3-934063-14-4

This book is only available in German at present. Publishers who are interested in publishing the book in English please contact: ravarebooks@gmail.com

www.bruno-b.ch/en

Enetechiel– essence

The third volume of the ENETECHIEL trilogy contains a concentrated summary of two intensive seminars. Everyday themes are explored from an in-depth transpersonal point of view. This volume invites readers to thoroughly examine and challenge well-established view-points. It showcases that Light and Love can only be experienced at a particular time and place: Now and internally.

»ENETECHIEL – essenz«
Ravare-Verlag 2005, Softcover, 121 S.
ISBN 3-9522382-2-8

*This book is only available in German at present.
Publishers who are interested in publishing the book
in English please contact: ravarebooks@gmail.com*

www.bruno-b.ch/en